Fashionable Clothing
from the Sears Catalogs
Mid 1940s

Tina Skinner & Lindy McCord

Schiffer Publishing Ltd

4880 Lower Valley Road, Atglen, PA 19310 USA

Contributors

Managing Editor - Tina Skinner

Editor - Lindy McCord

Photographer - Jenna Palecko Schuck

Designer - John Cheek

Cover Design - Bruce Waters

Designed by John P. Cheek
Type set in Zurich Ex BT/Zurich BT

ISBN: 0-7643-1858-6
Printed in China
1 2 3 4

Images used in this book are from the Sears Catalogs © Sears, Roebuck and Co., and are used with permission.

Fall/Winter 1943-44
7, 8, 9, 11, 10, 12, 13, 14, 15, 16, 21, 25, 27, 29, 30, 31, 35, 36, 37, 49, 51, 53, 57, 58, 59, 60, 64, 66, 68, 70, 91, 100, 103, 105, 106, 107, 108, 109, 115, 120, 121, 122, 124, 127, 128, 128A, 128C, 139F, 139H, 157D, 166, 167, 177, 179, 181, 186, 195, 207, 235, 238, 253, 291, 293, 3, 313, 321, 343, 345, 348, 349, 376, 394C, 396, 399, 411, 415, 419, 426, 433, 433C, 441, 449, 456, 465, 469, 486, 488, 505, 519, 529, 531

Spring/summer 1944
3, 5, 7, 8, 9, 10, 12, 14, 19, 27, 31, 34A, 34D, 34F, 34G, 35, 36, 37, 37, 38, 51, 55, 58, 60, 62, 73, 74, 76E, 77, 078, 79, 81, 88, 89, 90, 91, 92, 93, 96, 98, 99, 100, 103a, 109a, 124, 145B, 149, 150, 153, 154, 155-157, 164, 179, 189, 191, 193, 197, 199, 201, 203, 204, 207, 211, 213, 217, 219-223, 223, 225,227, 250, 251, 253, 254, 256, 259, 260, 263, 264,266, 267, 281, 294A, 294C, 295, 299, 301, 305, 307, 311, 315, 318, 324, 324B, 325, 327, 330, 331, 333, 337, 340, 345, 353, 354, 355, 358, 359, 361, 368, 371G, 376, 377, 383, 390A

Fall/winter 1944-45
4, 5, 7, 8, 9, 10, 11, 13, 15, 16, 18, 20, 23, 25, 27, 29, 38, 40, 44, 46, 47, 49, 54, 55, 57, 67, 68C, 73, 74, 75, 81, 85, 88, 94, 96, 97, 98, 99, 100, 101,102a, 115, 119, 121-125, 125C, 125D, 127, 128, 129, 130, 139, 141, 142, 151B, 173, 194, 213, 218, 219, 277, 278, 282, 28A, 28C, 28G, 296, 298, 300, 303, 305, 309, 316G, 325, 327, 329, 353, 357, 358, 367, 367B,375, 378, 381, 391, 391BL, 391R, 393, 395, 397,404C, 40B, 40E, 411, 415, 417, 418, 423-427,428,443, 444, 445, 451, 452, 452A, 453, 455, 479H, 482

Spring/Summer 1945
2, 3, 4, 5, 6, 7, 8, 10, 18-24, 25, 26, 27, 28, 29, 30, 32-66, 68, 69, 70, 72, 73, 77, 79, 81, 89, 91, 93, 95, 97C, 97D, 97E, 97F, 99, 100, 105, 111, 113A, 113B, 117, 119, 145, 147, 157, 163, 166, 171, 176-178, 201, 204-224, 227, 243, 267, 268-270, 271, 273, 275, 279, 281, 289, 303, 311, 317, 319, 325, 329, 331, 335, 343, 345, 347, 348, 350, 351BL, 351TL, 352, 353, 354, 365, 367, 369, 371, 373, 375-377, 379, 380-382, 387, 401, 411, 415, 417, 419, 422, 429, 439, 452, 453

Fall/winter 1945-46
3, 9, 12, 16, 22, 23, 25, 30, 32, 36-60, 65, 67, 71, 81, 87, 97, 115, 125, 126, 129, 131, 135, 139, 196, 199, 200, 207, 233, 276, 277, 279, 281, 283, 284

Published by Schiffer Publishing Ltd.
4880 Lower Valley Road
Atglen, PA 19310
Phone: (610) 593-1777; Fax: (610) 593-2002
E-mail: info@schifferbooks.com

Please visit our web site catalog at **www.schifferbooks.com**
We are always looking for people to write books on new and related subjects. If you have an idea for a book please contact us at the above address.

This book may be purchased from the publisher.
Include $3.95 for shipping.
Please try your bookstore first.
You may write for a free catalog.

In Europe, Schiffer books are distributed by
Bushwood Books
6 Marksbury Ave.
Kew Gardens
Surrey TW9 4JF England
Phone: 44 (0) 20 8392-8585; Fax: 44 (0) 20 8392-9876
E-mail: Bushwd@aol.com
Free postage in the U.K., Europe; air mail at cost.

Contents

Introduction

Here is yet another exciting book that provides a pictorial exploration of fashions from the Sears-Roebuck catalogs in the mid-1940s. As America found itself thrown headfirst into World War II, concerned and patriotic citizens wanted to do all they could for the war effort. But life went on, and even while America's bravest were fighting for their lives overseas, there was work to be done at home. Many American women left their domestic lives behind for manual labor and factory jobs. Trends in fashion reflected these changes. Women's fashions became "mannish" or "man-tailored," and pants and slack suits became ever more popular. New patterns were created for transforming men's suits into ladies' suits and women's dresses into children's clothing. Colors remained very patriotic, in army greens, and soldier or navy blues. Many styles, especially of children's clothing, imitated military uniforms. Sears also devoted several pages of catalog space to fabrics and patterns for thrifty women who sewed their own and their family's garments.

In 1942, the US Government War Production Board issued regulation L - 85, which regulated every aspect of clothing and restricted the use of natural fibers. Other fabrics, hosiery, dyes, and buttons were regulated as well. America thus turned to the production of artificial fibers, rayon being one of the most popular. Wool, although still a widely used natural material, became more expensive due to military needs. Clothing became more practical, more durable and rugged for working. Ration stamps were issued in limited amounts and required for amenities like leather shoes, handbags, and other accessories. This was not to deprive Americans of their real needs, but to make more certain that they got a fair share of the country's goods. Sanforized was a trademark meaning that the fabric could not shrink more than one percent, for lasting wear. It was applied not only to denim but also to all washables including work clothes, sportswear, housedresses, slips, pajamas, etc.

But even with the restrictions and limitations on clothing of this time, and the trend towards more masculine styles, women still felt the need to exert their femininity. More ruffles found their way to skirt hems, necklines, and waists. Gored, gathered, and A-line skirts were topped with soft, feminine blouses. Blouses donned bows at the center-front neckline and might sport full or puffy sleeves. Collars were cut generously full, in Peter Pan, scalloped, and traditional pointed shirt-collar designs. Lace also accentuated blouses around the neckline. Men's and women's clothing alike was "expertly tailored" for a proper, fine, finished look. In a time known as the "Big Band" era, where swing dancers and Lindy-hoppers twirled the night away, people tried to maintain high spirits amidst the horrors that faced the world. As the mid-1940s transitioned into post-war relief, the fashions would begin to change, becoming bolder, more outrageous, and more exciting. One of Sears' goals was to emphasize, especially to America's youth, the importance of "living it up" and having fun while sporting the latest fashions and styles, even in times of strife.

Original catalog language was abridged in the following captions, and a suggested price range for today's vintage clothing market is provided in brackets. These prices are meant only as a guideline, and the true value of the item is gauged by its condition, the interest and demand for the item in the current fashion world, and most notably, the significance it has to the collector.

Ann Barton. Sears Famous $4.98 shirtfrock. Good quality alpaca-type rayon. [$5-15] *Fall/winter 1943-44*

Women's Fashions

Dress Up

Extra value and service in these extra smart year rounders. Mallinson's Calvalcade, a rayon crepe, 2-piece dress, gored skirt, ruffled plaid collar and edges. Peg pocketed shirtfrock, detachable taffeta bow cuffs. Button front shirtfrock. Each $7 [$5-15] *Fall/winter 1943-44*

"Twill Tour"… warm rayon flannel. Two-piece suit dress, trim and smart 6-gore skirt. Wear jacket alone or with shirt or sweater. Fly front dress, buttons to hem. Set-in belt on front fullness. $10. [$5-15] *Fall/winter 1943-44*

Mallison's famous rayon crepe… so smart, yet so simple, you'll feel dressed for any occasion whether it's daytime or gaytime. Two-tone front fullness dress, Two-piece dress, stiched back, pressed open seams, taped 2-inch hems, smooth shoulder pads. $10 [$5-15] *Fall/winter 1943-44*

Botany… 100% virgin wool flannel. Two all-occasion classics, richly warm. 2-piece suit dress with convertible collar. $12.98 [$10-15] Shirtfrock, button fly-front, convertible collar. Leather belt. $9.98. [$25-35] *Fall/winter 1943-44*

Simple, soft-of-line dresses with important embroidery details. Fagoting outlines pastel yoke of two-piece dress. Sears-exclusive Contour-Closure rayon alpaca-type crepe. Colors: Black with pink yoke, navy with blue yoke. $8. [$10-15] Detachable dickey dress. For variety, replace crisp white dickey with a fluffy, ruffly one. Colors: Cadet blue, black. $7. [$5-10] *Fall/winter 1943-44*

Have you always wanted the flattery of luxurious velvet? V-neck dress, self appliqué and buttons, back gored skirt. Colors: black, wine. Cross draping of rayon transparent velvet. It also serves to slenderize. Body of dress is 100% wool. $10. [$20-30] *Fall/winter 1943-44*

Sears Super Values, famous $4.98 dresses. The long-sleeved pleated success, one piece with little pleatings down waist front and around slash pockets. Saucy bow neckline. The tuck-in two-piecer, one of the rising stars of fashion. Wear the bowed blouse with suits, too. Good quality rayon. [$3-5] *Fall/winter 1943-44*

Fashion's answer to your desire for something light and bright. Front-fullness dress, perfect background for varied accessories. Pouch pocket two-piece suit dress, figure-flattering top. Wear with blouses or dickies. Colors: Gold, pine aqua, rosewood. $10-12. [$5-15] *Fall/ winter 1943-44*

Basic styles to see you through the busiest morn-to-midnight schedule in good taste. Perky pleats, tiny darts give jacket a saucy line. Detachable white checked rayon taffeta collar, cuffs. Shirred bodice dress-up casual one piece dress. White flowers and cuffs dramatize it. Side torso buttons, wide self belt, back gored skirt gives figure flattery. $7 each. [$5-10] *Fall/winter 1943-44*

Softly done dresses that are right anywhere, anytime... Dressy casual dress with matching rayon taffeta ruching around collar. All around gored skirt. Colors: Forest green or soldier blue. Basic V dress with matching embroidery, flower trim. Colors: Soldier blue, rosewine. $8. [$15-20] *Fall/winter 1943-44*

Navy-with-white, Frankly's Rosita Rayon, a sure sign of spring and first choice for Easter. $8. [$5-15] *Spring/summer 1944*

Frothy, beautiful cotton nets in a wonderful style and color selection for the romantic new fashions America loves this year. Striped, dotted, plain, and floral flocked netting available. Under $1 per yard. *Spring/summer 1944*

Dress-up or casual 2 piece suit dresses. Sprightly style with a talent for double duty and a flair for flattery. Fine quality rayon crepe. Colors: Navy, black or aqua with self trim. $8. [$15-20] *Spring/summer 1944*

Choice wools for master-tailored suits. Hound's-tooth check, all wool tweed, skirt kick pleated in front and back. Black and white. Cardigan suit, Botany's new wool flannel. Comes in pastel yellow or sky blue. $19. [$25-35] *Spring/summer 1944*

Bemberg rayon, sheer print dress. $6.
[$5-15] *Spring/summer 1944*

Sears famous dresses by Ann Barton.
Mallinson's printed rayon Bermuda
cloth and Mimosa rayon shantung.
Two-piece, shirtfrock, and button front
styles available in bold, colorful prints.
$5. [$5-15] *Spring/summer 1944*

Side drapery duet in rayon crepe. Feminine, slenderizing, flattering to all figures.
Available in solid or floral prints, red, black, or powder blue. $8. [$10-20] *Spring/
summer 1944*

Sequins on Mallinson's "Whirlaway" rayon crepe. The glamour-glitter of sequins adds charm for dine-and-dance fashions. Basque dress with clusters of sequins available in royal blue, black, or gold. Two-piece with button front top available in brown with pastel blue or black with pastel rose. $10. [$20-30] *Fall/winter 1944-45*

Clever dresses, in Pacific's wool crepe or Mallinson's rayon "Whirlaway" designed to make you look taller and slimmer. $9-10. [$10-20] *Fall/winter 1944-45*

Stunzi's "Elissa" rayon crepe suit dress is a No. 1 favorite in two-piecers. Comfortable in fit because they're scaled especially for fuller figures, black and purple. $9. [$10-20] *Fall/winter 1944-45*

Man-tailored link-button suits in all new wools. For a strict look, choose the all wool worsted striped suit in black or navy. To be more feminine, take the satin bound all wool crepe in black. Both jackets are fully lined with rayon. $17-19. [$35-45] *Fall/winter 1944-45*

Every season, women look to Sears for a new two piece suit dress… to count on as their best outfit, for that well groomed, ensemble look. The Stunzi's "Elissa" rayon crepe suit dress, with fresh white trim at the throat and sleeves and passementerie pockets, is the perfect Easter costume, navy blue. $9. [$10-20] *Spring/summer 1945*

Searspride cottons and cotton mixtures. Seersucker coat dress, buttons up front. Perfect for all day, everyday wear. $2.79. Floral peg-top dress, popular because of its soft femininity. $2.79. Checked gingham shirtfrock, the style that can't be beat for all-around comfort and becomingness. Front pleated, black gored skirt for swing; rounded yoke for vestee effect. $3. [$1-5] *Fall/winter 1943-44*

Donegal-type part wool tweed suit. Mannish 3-button jacket with notched collar and gored back, skirt cut with six gores and two box pleats, front and back. $11. [$25-35] *Fall/winter 1943-44*

Dressmaker suit with detachable black Persian lamb fur buttons. Jacket lined with Earl-Glo rayon crepe, softly fitted with waistline darts, four gores in back, black. $20. Man-tailored style suit, wool worsted. Collar, fronts, lapels reinforced with shape-retaining canvas. Jacket seamed down center-back, navy blue or black, each with white pinstripe. $17. [$40-50 each] *Fall/winter 1943-44*

The fly front-effect dress, slenderizing, easy to wear line. Detachable white dickey. Colors: Gray, soldier blue, rosewine. $5. [$5-15] *Fall/winter 1943-44*.

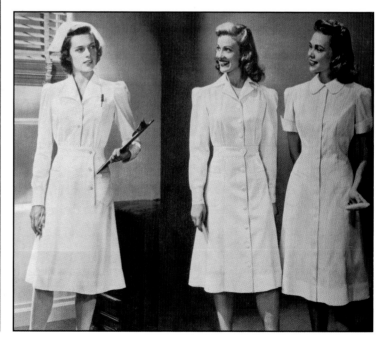

Professional uniforms for nurses, laboratory workers, or beauticians. Side button uniform with yoke back. Detachable fresh water pearl stud buttons. White only. Button front uniform, plated yoke back, 6-gore skirt. Detachable pearl buttons. Princess uniform with fly front, buttoned to below waist. Wear with or without belt. $2-4. [$5-10] *Fall/winter 1943-44*.

Sears heavy duty sanforized work clothes. Seersucker or poplin set-in waistband button front dress, designed for utility. Button-front work dress, good looking enough to wear to and from work as well as on the job. Belt stitched at back, loose in front. Built for robust wear. Blue or white. $3. [$5-10] *Fall/winter 1943-44*

Fine quality rayon dresses for women, nicely detailed, well made to serve you far into the future. French-type rayon crepe, fancy pockets dress, scalloped V-neck, and white lace and organdy styles. $5. [$5-10] *Fall/winter 1943-44*

Trimline fashions designed to slim you. Dress-up shirtfrock dress, sharply front pleated, back gored skirt completes "tall and narrow" look. Rayon alpaca-type crepe. $7. Printed shirtwaist dress, easy hanging, easy to wear. Spun rayon with neat Velveray print. $4. Popular button-front dress is the dress you'll live in. Spun rayon fabric. $3. [$10-15] *Fall/winter 1943-44*

Work dresses, easy to slip on, easy to iron, easy on the purse. Comfortable, cotton button front coat dresses, solid or striped. Magirap apron dress, reversible fronts to look fresher much longer. Full cut, comfortable to wear alone or over dresses. $2. [$5-15] *Fall/winter 1943-44*

Princess button-front spun rayon slenderizing rayon mixture dress. Colors: luggage brown with beige, navy with light blue. $3. [$5-15] *Fall/winter 1943-44*

Slimming details, fine fabrics are trimline features. Sheer rayon and cotton mixes, all-around gored skirts. All-purpose shirtfrocks achieve figure-slimming magic. $4-9. [$5-15] *Spring/summer 1944*

Scroll trimmed button front dress, or 2-piece suit dress, front tie, set in belted jacket. Both made from finest quality rayon. Dress in luggage brown, navy, or red with white trim. Suit dress available in clover green as well. $6-7. [$5-15 each] *Spring/summer 1944*

Nurses, lab workers, and beauticians uniforms. Available in white or copen blue with white collar and cuffs. $2-5. [$5-15] *Spring/summer 1944*

18

Suit dresses can be worn smartly under a coat or without one, depending on the weather. Rayon bengaline, duco-printed with a neat white design. In black only. Soft shirring at midriff of jacket, perfect for dining and dancing. Find it in navy blue, luggage brown, or leaf green with white dots. White braid embroidery, notched collar, and squared flaps. Comes in clover green or luggage brown with white trim. $5-7. [$10-20] *Spring/summer 1944*

Mallinson's Kameo sheer rayon provides year round comfort. Saw tooth edged dress has feathered front, back gored skirt. Navy with white trim, clover green with white trim. Side-button dress is a new, youthful fashion, with self belt and back gored skirt that has gathers in the front. Gray, sea aqua, melon rose. $5. [$5-15] *Spring/summer 1944*

Soft, dressy suits with beautiful lines. Smooth shoulders, curved waistlines, new necklines. Simply and shrewdly styled, they're good for all seasons. Two wool crepes with dazzle buttons, the other in fine striped rayon. All jackets lined with rayon. $15-19. [$30-40] *Spring/summer 1944*

Sturdy cotton work dresses, easy to slip into or iron. Youthful coverall, favorite button down front, and magirap apron dress. $2-3. [$5-15] *Spring/summer 1944*

Hand-screened flowers bloom brightly on Charmette's border print rayon jersey. $10. [$5-15] *Spring/summer 1944*

Conservative styles, longer skirts in the Gracious Lady spring wardrobe. $2-7.
[$5-15] *Spring/summer 1944*

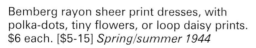

Bemberg rayon sheer print dresses, with
polka-dots, tiny flowers, or loop daisy prints.
$6 each. [$5-15] *Spring/summer 1944*

21

Shetland-type wool suit is a suit for town or country, A.M. or P.M., dressy or casual wear, depending on your accessories. Fine tailoring to give a good shoulderline, slimness through the middle, pastel beige, pastel blue, or lilac. $15-20. [$25-35] *Spring/summer 1944*

Comfortable dresses of "Super Charmalac," Charmette's new even-weave fabric has a woolly warmth because it's part aralac, part rayon. Excellent for all-purpose wear. $4. [$5-15] *Fall/winter 1944-45*

Finest rayon gabardine dresses in the most fashionable styles and colors. Favored by Hollywood designers. Multi-stitched button front dress and saddle bag pocket dress are two styles not to be missed. Available in pine green, gold, and violet. $9. [$5-15] *Fall/winter 1944-45*

Tebilized rayon flannel dresses are firm-textured and weighty, giving the appearance of costly English wool. Surplice fly-front dress sports shoulder flaps and tucks for a swagger look of a trench coat. The bib yoke shirtfrock has the easy comfort you like, with bloused fullness. Available in lemon yellow, violet, and aqua green. $9. [$5-15] *Fall/winter 1944-45*

The button-front uniform, No. 1 choice of active nurses. Action-built with pleated back shoulder yoke to give easily as you move. $2-5. [$5-15] F*all/winter 1944-45*

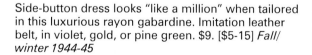

Side-button dress looks "like a million" when tailored in this luxurious rayon gabardine. Imitation leather belt, in violet, gold, or pine green. $9. [$5-15] *Fall/winter 1944-45*

Sanforized-shrunk work clothes for factory or farm. Built rugged like a man's work clothes… practical and dependable. Navy blue, dark blue, and brown. $2. [$30-40] *Fall/winter 1944-55*

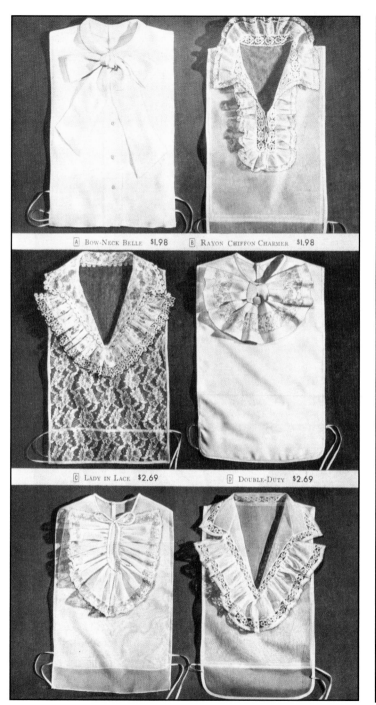

A BOW-NECK BELLE $1.98   B RAYON CHIFFON CHARMER $1.98

C LADY IN LACE $2.69   D DOUBLE-DUTY $2.69

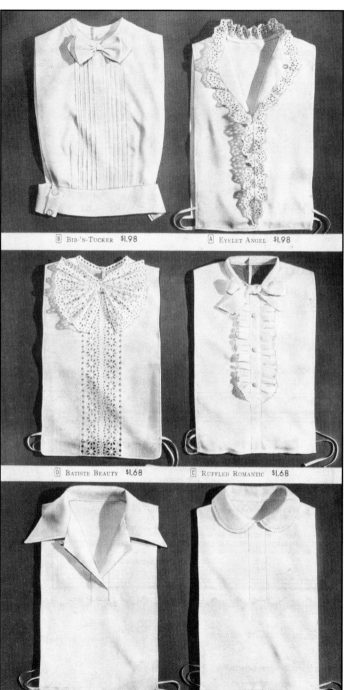

B BIB-'N-TUCKER $1.98   A EYELET ANGEL $1.98

D BATISTE BEAUTY $1.68   C RUFFLED ROMANTIC $1.68

Smartest dickies, the fine frills and lovely laces every feminine heart fancies in dainty new designs. All accented with bows, ribbons, and ruffles. $2-3. [$5-10] *Fall/winter 1944-45*

25

Button-trimmed cottons and rayons. Various styles and colors. $3-4. [$10-20] *Fall/winter 1944-45*

All-purpose favorites in rayon. Button front dress with clover trim festooned around buttons. Basic V-neck flatters all sizes and is versatile. The suit effect dress has all around peplum for youthful, two-piece look. $5.49 each. [$10-20] *Fall/winter 1944-45*

↑ G Knife-Pleated Skirt $3.98   ↑ D Wool and Rabbit's Hair Jersey Dirndl $4.98   ↑ E Pacific All Wool Crepe $4.98

ALL PAGE 5 . . . . . DRESSES

Kerrybrooke's finely tailored skirts in part wool and all wool. Color takes the lead, both in striking solo shades and in the youthful harmony of plaids. $3-6. [$5-15] *Fall/winter 1944-45*

Frankly's Pacalon, a good quality rayon alpaca-type fabric is worthy of the fine making that goes into Sears famous $4.98 dresses. Varied styles available in navy, cherry rose, aqua, pearl gray, and black. Add a mandarin pompadour hat, Chelton beret, or a halo beret to top off the outfit. Hats: $2 each. [$5-15] *Fall/winter 1944-45*

Draped dresses of "Cavalcade" rayon crepe. Torso folds and tiny button-opening down the front follow lines of figure to show off lovely curves. Colors: black and aqua. Cascade side ripple serves as clever hip hider, and makes you look taller. Colors: Black or brown. $8. [$15-25] *Fall/winter 1944-45*

Dressmaker suits in doeskin-effect flannel has that made-for-you look. Shirt-collar suit is dressed up with pockets made of curly black wool, cotton backed, resembling Persian lamb. The cardigan suit has long darts for soft figure-flattering fullness. $19. [$35-45]
Fall/winter 1944-45

This is the year for the soft suit. Chalk-white stripes are used figure-wisely for the cardigan suit in a rich rayon suiting. Well cut skirt with gores for smart lines, dark gray-and-white, dark brown-and-white. Brighton suiting, 70% rayon, 30% aralac… a crisp stay-fresh fabric for the 3-button classic. Available in Lime (light green), American beauty (bluish red), and medium blue. $13-17. [$25-35] *Spring/summer 1945*

Suit-dresses rate high with well-groomed women for their planned-costume look. The Labtex butcher rayon saw-tooth edged suit dress comes in bright green and cocoa brown, and edging narrows down from shoulder to jacket bottom for slimming shapeliness. $8. [$20-30] *Spring/summer 1945*

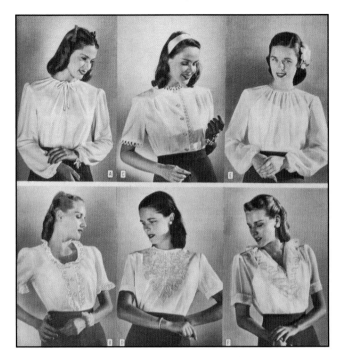

Dressy styles of Sears finest blouses, quality rayons. Drawstring neckline (yellow, white, bright green), cardigan neck blouse with loop trimming for dressy effect, round neck blouse with full sleeves gathered at wrist, low oval neck blouse in fine cotton batiste with cotton eyelet embroidery in ruffle edges at neckline, embroidered round neck blouse in rayon crepe with rich white scroll embroidery, and V-neck blouse in sheer rayon, yoke front with gathers. White only. $3-4. [$10-20] *Spring/summer 1945*

Ⓐ THE TRAPUNTO SUIT shown in medium green $21.50
Also comes in medium brown and medium blue, below

Ⓑ TUCKED SHOULDER SUIT shown in fuchsia (purplish red) $18.98
Also comes in navy blue and aqua blue, below

SEARS MN / PAGE 69 / SUITS

Dressmaker suits, finely detailed in pure new woolens. Trapunto suit in rich smooth-finish all wool with fine detailing on jacket (medium green, medium blue, medium brown). Tucked-shoulder suit in all wool crepe comes in jewel tone colors (fuchsia, aqua blue, navy blue), and cardigan jacket closes with bright buttons. Skirt hangs slim and straight as all new-fashion skirts do. $19-22. [$25-35] *Spring/summer 1945*

Softly detailed, all season dresses of fine quality rayon alpaca-type fabric. Berlinger products have a national reputation for lasting beauty and luxurious drape. Two-tone suit dress, youthfully styled with scalloped dotted panel on jacket, creates thinning effect. Navy blue or black with white polka dots. $9. [$5-15] *Spring/summer 1945*

Like gaiety, charm of color? Get all you want in these two-tone prints. The loop print suit dress, shirred, figure-following jacket. Made of better quality, smooth rayon crepe. Medium gray-and-white, light blue-and-brown, fuchsia and black. $9. [$5-15] *Spring/summer 1945*

Velveray-printed bengaline, a lustrous ribbed rayon, lends elegance, texture interest to simplicity of classic suit dress. Frankly's glamour, a firm-weave rayon crepe, is specially selected to give good hang to soft-line suit dress. Rosette-fluffs of eyelet embroidery on detachable dickey offer springtime freshness. $8 each. [$15-25] *Spring/summer 1945*

Good or best quality, soft monotone short-coat and collarless wool suit, available in medium green, gold, or medium blue. Entire outfit: $23 each. [$50-75] *Spring/summer 1945*

Berlinger's alpaca-type fabric is a medium weight, evenly-textured sheer. Just right for now, especially in spring blues, not too light in body for winter. Button front dress has curving embroidery, slimming column of buttons, neat duco-printed design (deep blue, dark green, black), side drape wrap dress has flared drapery cascading from surplice v-neckline, which gives movie-star slimness (navy blue, black, deep rose), and the v-neck dress has sleek midriff topped by rayon sheer bodice, braid-embroidered (medium blue, black). $9. [$15-25] *Spring/summer 1945*

Zig-zag suit in soft monotone wool has zig-zag banding to call attention to a smart shoulderline. Dark gold, medium blue, medium green, and cocoa (medium brown). $23. [$15-25] *Spring/summer 1945*

31

Charmette's even-weave fabric, wearable year round. Shirtfrocks in crisp rayon sharkskin (white, red-white checks, medium blue-white checks), or rayon sandgrain dresses, light in weight with interesting pebble weave and slight luster. $4 each. [$5-15] *Spring/summer 1945*

All-year casuals in a fresh mood. Accent on light, bright colors, style newness. Round neck dress of Stunzi's rayon gabardine comes in aqua blue, beige, and melon. The petal-collared dress with *Talon* slide fastener features scallops that go from neck to hips. Available in soft gold, melon, and aqua blue. $8. [$5-15] *Spring/summer 1945*

Two-piece suits in all wool striped flannel or wool-and-rayon checked tweed. Lots of style, lots of wear, famous Sears quality in smart tailored fashions. Tweed jacket has small lapels, rounded club collar. 4-gore skirt with inverted pleat front and back. Available in black and white. White stripes add to the look of slenderness in the fine gray two piece with long lapels, and slim man-tailored lines. $13-15. [$35-45] *Fall/winter 1945-46*

Far left:
A popular American classic, the long loose boxy cardigan is casual and easy to wear. Necks are smooth ribbed and tapered sleeves fit better. $3-6 [$30-50] *Fall/winter 1943-44*

Left:
The long loose boxy pullover comes in Celanese rayon, fine virgin wool, and imported virgin zephyr wool. Bright, classic colors. Ribbed, flat-lying necklines and shaped armholes for freedom and fine fit. $2-5 [$30-50] *Fall/winter 1943-44*

Fine low-priced Slacks and Riding Wear. Hard working washable slacks, roomy and well fitted. Sturdy cotton twill in navy, or sanforized-shrunk dart back denims with deep slash pockets. Both $1.98. Trimly tailored cotton calvary twill saddle pants, knee guards, bar-tacked pockets, chamois lined crotch. Jodhpurs with suede knee guards, lined interior. Both $4. [$5-20] *Fall/winter 1943/44*

Dressy rayon blouses. Striped blouse with cut sleeves, swirl striping in red and white or blue and white. Deep-throated rayon crepe with a wingspread of ruffles in cotton Val-type lace. Tucked-front blouse in fine rayon crepe goes wonderfully with everything. The embroidered eyelet has ruffles peeking out from the neckline and sleeves. $2-3. [$5-15] *Fall/winter 1943-44*

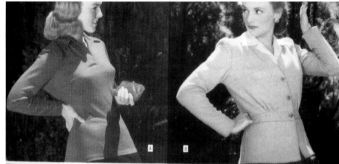

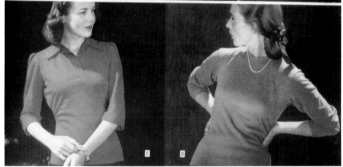

Knit fabrics are beautifully used for warm, flattering sports classics. Long pullover, torso blouse, "twillone" jacket, and a round-necked skirt are too pretty to hide under jackets, but their necklines are marvelous for suits. $2-5 [$5-15] *Fall/winter 1934-44*

Midriff button-front dress in navy with white dots. Opens flat for speedy ironing. $1.98. Paisley button-front dress, gathers at waist for working freedom. Comes in assorted paisley prints. $1.79. [$5-15] *Fall/winter*

Heavy duty sanforized-shrunk work clothes for factory or farm. Coveralls, jackets, slacks, overalls, shirts, and slack suits. $1-3. [$10-30] *Spring/summer 1944*

Cloud print shirtfrock of Mimosa Shantung, a rayon fabric. Ruffles around the sleeves and slashed side set-in pockets, buttons to waist. Flower print button front dress of Bermuda cloth, a rayon broadcoth with a look of silk. Back gored skirt, set-in, tie front belt. White-printed luggage brown, melon rose, leaf green, or azure blue. $5. [$5-15] *Spring/summer 1944*

Fine Searspride cotton dresses. Tie-front two-piece suit dress of woven seersucker, trim fitting. Frill ruffled shirtfrock of woven plaid gingham. Band trimmed button front dress enjoys the striking contrast of sharp white against red or blue. $4-5. [$5-15] *Spring/summer 1944*

Having budget trouble? Then sew your own! Fabric for complete wardrobe costs under $20. Rayon striped jersey, smart shantung texture cotton-and-rayon, white sharkskin, pin-wale corduroy, and herringbone fabrics available for attractive dresses and outerwear. [$5-15] *Spring/summer 1944*

Casual skirts, attractive colors. Wool and rayon crepe styles, multi-gored for a graceful, dressy look. $2-6. [$5-15] *Spring/summer 1944*

Pinafore parade. Button-back cottons serve well as dresses in colorful and lively prints, stripes, and solids. $2-3. [$5-10] *Spring/summer 1944*

Trimline washable cottons for women and stout women. Floral, striped, dotted, and printed styles in sturdy cotton. $2. [$5-10] *Spring/summer 1944*

Casual sweater favorites. Jumbo knit cardigan in red, yellow, and copen blue. All wool lady pilgrim, famous V-neck classic in navy or wine. $2-4. [$30-50] *Spring/summer 1944*

Kerrybrooke riding clothes, famous for style and quality. Cotton calvary twill jodhpurs and saddle pants, or sanforized mercerized cotton gabardine prairie pants. $3-5. [$5-20] *Spring/summer 1944*

Sears famous Ann Barton dresses. Bib-ruffle button front style made of French-type rayon crepe. Ruching-trimmed dress combines simple, classic styling with flattering softness. $5. [$5-10] *Spring/summer 1944*

A shirtfrock does wonders for any size figure. Set-in belt, buttons to waist in front. Button front shirtfrock is a first choice for carefree comfort and dateless charm. Both rayon shantung, in maize, sea aqua, and rosepink. $5. [$5-10] *Spring/summer 1944*

Crown tested French-type rayon crepe in fall-winter colors with white polka dots. Another super value from Sears famous Ann Barton collection. Styles include tucked bosom dress, shirtwaist dress, and button front dress. Cocoa brown, navy, pine green, violet, red. $5. [$5-15] *Fall/winter 1944-45*

Cardigans double for jackets or blouses, and top skirts and slacks. Waffle design, v-neck, jacquard knit, chenille vestee, jumbo knit torso fashion styles each have character and flair. Available in fall colors. $5-7. [$15-20] *Fall/winter 1944-45*

Apron assortment! Take cover under pretty cottons while you work. Floral pinafore, stripped bib-topper, ric-rac trimmed, and halter-neck coverall styles come in assorted colors and prints. All aprons have front pockets. $1-2. [$10-20] *Fall/winter 1944-45*

Jersey blouses in bright colors, warm and either all wool or rayon. V-neck blouse, torso blouse, tie-neck, and round neckline go well with any fall costume. $2-4. [$5-15] *Fall/winter 1944-45*

Everyday luxable rayon-and-cotton dresses. Scalloped tuck button front dress you slip into easily. Coin dot button front dress with loose tie belt. Scalloped collar adds softness to floral print shirtfrock. Tucked bosom, contrasting whip-stitching and buttons add zest to all-occasion shirtfrock. $3.49. [$5-15] *Fall/winter 1944-45*

Styles are sweet and pretty… with the simplicity of wear-everywhere good taste. Floral print bow trimmed dress with new rounded neckline and back gored skirt. Available in white with aqua blue and fuchsia, or pink ground with aqua blue and white flowers. $9. [$5-15] *Spring/summer 1945*

Women's all-occasion dresses of "Crownella"… a crown rayon fabric. Scalloped leaf print shirtfrock (floral on light blue ground, gray ground, or medium green ground), surplice floral shirtfrock (brown on light blue ground, aqua blue on pink ground, medium green on gray), sweetheart neck dress with plastic buckles in floral print (rust florals on aqua, rose florals on gray, gold florals on light blue), and button front shirtfrock with medallion florals and bows on bodice (medium blue, medium green). $4-5. [$5-15] *Spring/summer 1945*

Aprons are grand clothes savers! Washable cotton aprons with halter necks, assorted designs. Tie back. Come in assorted cheery designs. 40¢-80¢. [$10-20] *Fall/winter 1943-44*

Golf and tennis classics...full cut for freedom of action. Misses' cotton tennis blouse and tennis shorts with pocket on left side. $2. [$5-15] Visor with adjustable headband, under $1. [$2-5] *Spring/summer 1945*

Becoming styles, tailored and dressy rayon blouses. Drawstring neck in crepe (white), jacket blouse in fine, firm-weave rayon with wide revers and yoke front (white), jabot blouse with bow in rayon crepe, shirred self fabric ruffle down front (white), and gay floral print in sheer rayon, classic shirtwaist style with long, full sleeves. $2 each. [$5-15] *Spring/summer 1945.*

Women's riding wear. Expertly tailored for riding comfort with lines designed to flatter your figure. Rayon gabardine shirts, part wool frontier style pants, chino-twill jodhpurs. $4-10. [$5-20] *Fall/winter 1945-46*

Lingerie

Designed to prevent panties from riding up, this corset, by a famous California designer, is stretchy and comfortable. $4.50. [$5-10] *Fall/winter 1943-44*

A pair of red sports Flatterees for the active woman. Shirts have plain Dutch neck. Comfortable but warm and supportive. Short sleeve or ankle length longs, $1-2. Brief panties, 69¢ each, or 3 for $2. [$5-10] *Fall/winter 1943-44*

Charmode classic slips come in two lengths, short and regular, and are soft and smooth, with lovely wide lace at the top and bottom. Comes in tea rose and white. $3. [$2-5] *Fall/winter 1943-44*

Charmode NU-BACK deluxe foundations. Masterfully cut, beautifully designed of luxurious fabrics. Makes the larger figure that needs firm, all-over support look lovelier and trimmer. Elegantly styled of gorgeous rayon and cotton brocade with beautiful net-lined cotton lace bra tops. $8-12. [$5-10] *Fall/winter 1943-44*

A Sears Super Value-Charmode classic nightgown made from finer fabrics to be soft, smooth, and lovely. They offer a favorite, simple style and shoulder straps shaped for a perfect fit. $2-4. [$2-5] *Fall/winter 1943-44*

Luxurious Charmode nightgowns. Made of soft cottons and rayon satin. $2-6. [$2-5] *Spring/summer 1944*

Charmode "Dia-trim" all-in-ones. Well boned. Available in nude color. $4-7. [$5-10] *Spring/summer 1944*

Rosetex sturdy knit rayon combinations. Bra top combination has smooth, figure conforming lines, ideal for under sports and play clothes. $1-2. The sleek slackster is the perfect garment to wear under overalls, defense uniforms, or slacks. Well made with fitted, double fabric bodice top. $1-2. [$5-10] *Spring/summer 1944*

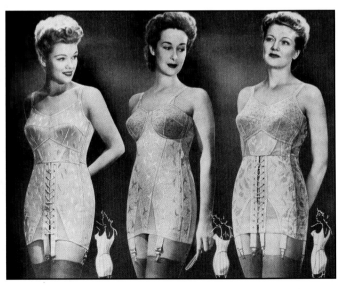

Charmode Nu-Back inner belt foundations. Luxurious fabrics plus the famous patented sliding back feature make these foundations first choice for comfort, control, and beauty. $8-12. [$5-10] *Spring/summer 1944*

Special feature co-ed panties and full figure panties. All designed of firm, curve-controlling fabrics with elastic inserts to give necessary release. Nude colors. $3-6. [$5-10] *Spring/summer 1944*

Pilgrim Flatter-ees panties and briefs. Designed for the modern, active woman who wants the utmost in comfort, trim fit, and durability. Made of cotton and rayon. Two lengths available. 30¢-90¢. [$5-10] *Fall/winter 1944-45*

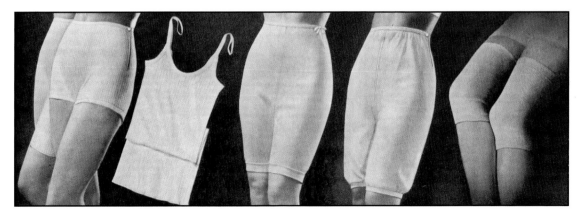

Charmode side hook girdles, so easily adjustable! Just pull the laces for better control. Slim and trim your figure. $2-4. [$5-10] *Spring/summer 1945*

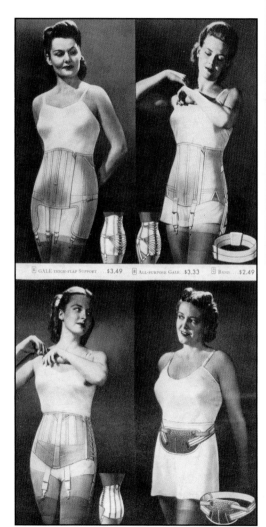

[A] GALE THIGH-FLAP SUPPORT...$3.49   [B] ALL-PURPOSE GALE...$3.33   [C] BAND...$2.49

Scientifically designed Gale supports, for smooth thigh, abdominal, and back support. $2-4. [$5-10] *Spring/summer 1945*

Maternity, nursing, and beauty bras. Made of lustrous rayon satin, and some cotton net. Made for all shaped and sized busts. $1-2. [$5-10] *Spring/summer 1945*

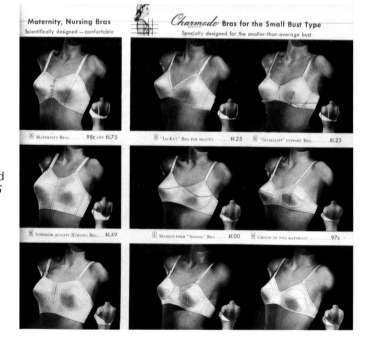

Maternity, Nursing Bras
Scientifically designed — comfortable

Charmode **Bras for the Small Bust Type**
Specially designed for the smaller-than-average bust

[A] MATERNITY BRAS...98¢ AND $1.75   [B] "LO-KUT" BRA FOR BEAUTY...$1.25   [C] "INVIZALIFT" SUPPORT BRA...$1.25

[D] SUPERIOR QUALITY NURSING BRA...$1.49   [E] MAIDEN-FORM "ADAGIO" BRA...$1.00   [F] CHOICE OF TWO MATERIALS...97¢

Charmode glamorous lightweight all-in-ones. Marvelous comfort and control, all or part elastic, entirely boneless. Quality and comfortable fabrics, clever designing, and youthfully styled bra tops mold your figure smartly. Available in nude color. $4-8. [$5-10] *Spring/summer 1945*

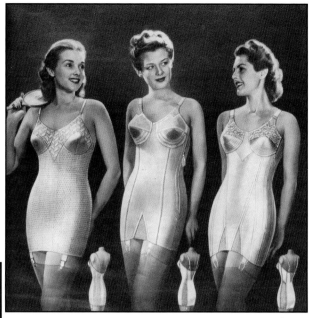

Royal purple hosiery… the sheerest, finest rayon stockings in two flattering styles- Service weight full fashioned stockings with fine, even seams, practical for work, fashionable for dress. Or skin-smooth bareleg style stockings favored by young moderns. Double tops, durable mercerized cotton feet. 50¢-$1 per pair. [$2-5] *Spring/summer 1945*

Sears famous classic slips. Strait-fit slip, better rayon crepe (white, tea rose), Perfec-fit slip, straight cut front and sides (white, navy blue, tea rose), tailored midriff slip in soft-filament rayon satin, creates slim lines (white, tea rose), and popular built up style in petal-soft rayon crepe. Fits trimly with smooth, figure conforming lines (tea rose, white). $1-2. [$2-5] *Spring/summer 1945*

49

Synthetic elastic panties and girdles with patented Cordtex tops for added comfort and support. $2-4. [$5-10] *Spring/summer 1945*

Softly tailored rayon slips. Best selling styles in durable, soft textured rayon fabrics. Fashioned for perfect fit… each a typical Sears value. $2 each. [$5-10] *Spring/ summer 1945*.

Housewear and Pajamas

Sears own flannelette Jamarettes, made of extra heavy, deeper napped, washable flannelette. Superbly tailored like men's pajamas. Smart plaid 'n plain style, and woven stripe. Colors: dusty blue, dusty rose, rose stripe, blue stripe. $2 [$5-10] *Fall/winter 1943-44*

Three lovely ladies lounge in comfy winter-warm knit cotton nightwear. Long sleeve gown and comfortable top and pants come in tea rose and blue. $1.59. "Puss 'n Boots" style top is cleverly cut and blousey with snug cuffs, trousers have comfy drawstring waist. Blue and coral. $2. [$5-10] *Fall/winter 1943-44*

Long-wearing, warm, tailored robes in gay colors. Corduroy, and flannel with suede-like texture. $6. Figure-flattering print house-coats. Bright, fashion-right for leisure hours. Dirndl style for year-round beauty, box pleated ruffles to give that glamorous, feminine look. $4. [$10-20] *Fall/winter 1943-44*

Warm, soft-as-down Bedjackets

Warm, soft-as-down bedjackets, in rich fluffy chenille, $2, or quilted rayon taffeta, $3.[$5-10; $25-30 for chenille] *Fall/winter 1943-44*

Bedtimers- new boudoir slippers. Rayon, satin, open toed, fur cuffed chenille styles. You'll like the relaxing comfort you get when your feet sink down on the soft and comfortable insoles. $1-3. [$5-10] *Fall/winter 1943-44*

Charmode cotton gowns. Fine cotton pinafore gown. You'll love the flattery of the fluffy ruffles and dainty cotton lace. Cotton voile is delightfully cool, marvelously serviceable. Bias cut; graceful bodice has ric-rac trim. $2-3. [$5-10] *Spring/summer 1944*

"Swirlaway" in chenille-gingham robes. Cozy and flattering, it's a housecoat hit. Colors: blue-and-white or red-and-white checks with white tufting. $5. [$80-100] *Spring/summer 1944*

Put your money in a quality robe like this and you've something you can wear and enjoy for years. Ara-ray flannel, a blend of aralac and spun rayon, keeps you comfortably warm and cozy. $14. [$10-20] *Fall/winter 1944-45*

Handsome robes for warmth and wear. Beacon cotton blanket cloth, ankle length, braid trim, ample overlap. Blue ground, wine ground. $6. [$80-100] *Fall/winter 1944-45*

53

Corduroy wrap robe and sueded rayon with soft downy surface help fight the chill on cold winter nights. $6-8. [$10-20] *Fall/winter 1944-45*

Gowns that are practical and pretty. The cotton crinkle crepe is soft, durable, stays daisy fresh after washing and never needs ironing. Fine imported cotton batiste gown is styled sweetly feminine in a flattering Victorian manner. $2-3. [$10-20] *Fall/winter 1944-45*

Easy-to-wash housecoats in cheerful colors, for misses, women… Sateen, colorful good quality in wrap style. Floral printed bengaline, cotton and rayon wrap style, piped in white. Floral cotton and rayon in young midriff style, pretty enough to serve as a hostess gown. $3-6. [$5-15] *Spring/summer 1945*

Rayon quilted robes in flower sprayed patterns, beautifully made of fine quality fabrics to keep you cozy and warm. Young, flattering styles for misses. Rayon twill robe with scalloped edges, deep lapels, and collar. Cut along princess lines in back; wide front overlap (light pink or light blue background). Rayon crepe robe with figure fitting bodice, becoming surplice neckline, front tie (white, tearose, light blue ground). Quilted shortie, dress length. Comfortable and convenient. $7-11. [$5-15] Fall/winter 1945

Outerwear

Kerrybrooke short coats are made to resist wind and weather. Warmth is stored up in their special fabrics and cotton kasha linings, and they're perfect for work or play. Made from water-repellent poplin, sturdy all wool melton cloth, or all wool plaid Mackinaw. $7-11. [$25-35] *Fall/winter 1943-44*

Fleece coats, wrap-tie style with button on belt and Earl-glo rayon lining. All wool fleece Balmacaan overcoat style, wide overlap closing, deep pockets. Welt seams throughout, pleat at back. $16. [$25-35] *Fall/winter 1943-44*

Leather jackets and shorties, warm, strong, wear-resistant leathers, velvety suede or smooth glossy capeskin. Snugly fitted shorties for warmth, fully lined. Wonderful for work. $8-13. [$35-45] *Fall/winter 1943-44*

Sears famous Chesterfields, the most popular style in years. Raglan-sleeved, Shetland-type wool in straight-line style, or fly-front in all wool overcoating. Handsome velveteen collars, high quality, rich and sturdy. Colors: Medium brown, red, cadet blue, or black. $17. [$30-40] *Fall/winter 1943-44*

Fine quality fur jackets and toppers, sable-dyed coney, silver fox, and skunk dyed styles. Each fluffy and luxurious, in 24, 30, or 36 inch lengths. $38-65. [$50-75] *Fall/winter 1943-44*

Kerrybrooke gabardine raincoats for women, and juniors too. Fine quality, made by men's tailors and "weather-sealed" by Impregnole, the laboratory certified showerproofing process. Balmacaan style with freedom-cut raglan sleeves, and Officer's coat, very military with its trench flap. Both in natural tan. $6-8. [$25-35] *Fall/winter 1943-44*

Year-round coats... removable rabbit fur linings. Tweed or fleece coats, styled for comfort and warmth. $30. [$20-30] *Fall/winter 1943-44*

Finest leather toppers, newest way to look smart, keep warm. Rich-smooth capeskin leather, plenty of dash in its swingy style, in black or luggage brown. Velvety suede leather with squared-off switched shoulders, in red, earth brown, or leaf green. $20. [$30-40] *Fall/winter 1943-44*

Five-button single breasted reefer jacket, designed to bring height and slenderness to the shorter figure. One button boxy coat with small round collar, graceful pretty front shirring is released from shoulder. Botany's all wool Karasham, Skinner's rayon satin lining in both. $22.50. [$20-30] *Fall/winter 1943-44*

Tweed coats, fine all wool herringbone. Well tailored and interlined. All wool overcoat, convertible collar, cut like a man's. All welt seamed, a pleat at back hemline, flat pockets. All wool reefer with velveteen collar, a fitted coat that's always extra warm with Skinner's rayon lining. $15. [$10-20] *Fall/winter 1943-44*

Opposites attract... color contrast is news for suits and coats. Checked tweed coat in brown-and-white or Shetland-type part wool in watermelon red. $11-15. [$10-20] *Spring/summer 1944*

Witness these coats. They have sparkle. They're fresh and new... and yet you'll not tire of them easily. Twin-button part wool twill, part rayon. Tuxedo box coat of self-striped bouclé. Rayon lining. Tucked reefer of all new wool crepe, gores give you fashionable slimness. Black or navy. $15-20. [$30-40] *Spring/summer 1944*.

Dressy twills bound in rayon satin. Popular box coat, back vent pleat. All wool or part wool. Twin button reefer, fitted and flared. Navy or black. $20-30. [$30-40] *Spring/summer 1944*.

Colorful coats designed to top everything you own. Big-buttoned corduroy, rich and velvety ribbed. Buttonless casual in fluffy fleece. 3-button casual in 100% Shetland-type wool. Chesterfield with flattering rayon velvet collar. $7-10. [$20-30] *Spring/summer 1944*

The wrap-tie wool coat is the pet of movie stars who call it their "cover-all coat" since it can be worn with slacks as well as dresses. You've perfection of fit when it's tied to your waistline. Sky blue, honey brown, or light beige, in three fine quality woolens. $13-20. [$25-35] *Spring/summer 1944*

The ever-popular Sears Chesterfield coat now comes in six beautiful fall colors: evergreen, dark brown, slate blue, cranberry red, black, and purple. The fabric is soft napped, smooth and hardy. Full rayon lining with sling straps of the same material for tossing over your shoulder at the first sign of warm weather. $23. [$20-30] *Fall/winter 1944-45*

Redgate soft monotone wool Chesterfield coat has rich rayon velvet detail that accents easy broad shoulders and tapers down to deep pockets. Slate blue, medium brown, or evergreen. $17.50. [$25-35] *Fall/winter 1944-45*

A man can tell you… there's nothing like a good warm overcoat, expertly tailored and wearable day in and out. The Balmacaan has a button-high collar to keep you warm, and the well-cut shoulders show off the casual easy lines you admire. Dark teal blue, dark brown. The Chesterfield has a new rounded look to its lapels, and rayon velvet at the neck. Black and navy. $32.50 [$25-35] *Fall/winter 1944-45*

Button-in linings for an all-year coat. Shed the windproof chamois leather lining to turn a warm winter coat into one that offers year round usefulness. The all wool monotone tweed Chesterfield with rayon velvet collar, and the Balmacaan, also all wool monotone tweed, come in dark soldier blue and brown. $29.98. [$20-40] *Fall/ winter 1944-45*

Warm winter coats go to new lengths for fashion rightness. The short cut coat falls just right to swing over suits and slacks. These coats sport the newest of trimmings… thick, silky rayon and cotton braid! All lined with rayon. $15-23. [$20-30] *Fall/winter 1944-45*

The Chesterfield is the No.1 coat of the year. $17.50. [$25-35] *Fall/winter 1944-45*

All wool fleece coats are bright, colorful, and warm. Wrap coat is one of the most sought after versions, set-in tie belt for a small drawn waist and raglan shoulders give that "Hollywood" look. The Balmacaan has all the crisp tailoring details you admire in a man's coat. The collar is flattering and feminine. Both come in slate blue, brown, and red. $23. [$25-35] *Fall/winter 1944-45*

THE TWIN-BUTTONED REEFER (shown in med. green) $17.98 and $24.98
Also comes in light soft blue, cocoa (medium brown), black, below

C THE CHESTERFIELD shown in cocoa, (med. brown) $17.98 and $24.98
Also comes in light soft blue, medium green, black, below

The boy coat in suede-like woolens. All wool or melton cloth fabrics, in dark brown, slate blue, or evergreen. $17-25. [$25-35] *Fall/winter 1944-45*

With persian lamb-like fabric of all wool face on cotton back, the cuff coat is the next best thing to a fur coat! Lines to flatter a woman's figure. Available in black. $30. [$25-35] *Fall/winter 1944-45*

Twin-buttoned reefer with new smoothed-out shoulder fold, inverted back pleat. Medium green, light soft blue, cocoa brown, and black. Chesterfield coat has a flange drape shoulderline and rayon velvet collar, same colors. Two qualities. $18-25. [$25-35] *Spring/summer 1945*

65

Kerrybrooke suit, coat in soft colorful wools. Colors: medium blue, medium green, medium brown. Two qualities. $15-20. [$50-75] *Spring/summer 1945*

All purpose coats in fine fabrics. Club-collared box coat in twill has a button trimmed flange that ends in concealed pockets. Fully rayon lined (navy blue, black). Twin-buttoned coat in soft, casual monotone wool for a slim, tapered line (medium blue, medium brown, black, navy blue). Boy coat in popular casual weave, all wool. Pencil line seam from shoulders to hip. Young, boxy lines, carved lapels (medium blue, medium brown, black, medium green). $17-18. [$25-35] *Spring/summer 1945*

Slim, trim fitted reefer. Favored for its flattering lines. Heart lapels, vertical pockets. Young, well cut boy coat. A first-choice with women year after year. Both in herringbone tweed, soft-finish monotone wool, or velvety suede-like all wool. $15-25. [$25-35] *Spring/summer 1945*

66

Dressy coats with luxury details. Simple, basic coats are touched with details headlined by topflight fashion designers. Softened, flattering lines. Slimming, insures easy fit. Rayon lined. Tapered reefer style, navy or black. Cardigan tuxedo style in wool crepe, slimming pencil-line trapunto from dropped shoulder yoke. $17-23. [$25-35] *Spring/summer 1945*

Dyed coney coats. Full draped tuxedo, dressy looking. Converts to closed collarless style. Available in platinum gray dyed or light brown dyed coney. Fitted princess coat, gay, small-wasted flaring silhouette does wonders for the figure. Beautifully worked border treatment. Available in platinum blue-gray or light brown. $82.50. [$60-80] *Fall/winter 1945-46*

Ready for a smart appearance in any weather…trim tailored-to-perfection raincoats, classic trench style, or softly feminine dressmaker coat. Medium tan, navy blue, or black. $14-15. [$15-20] *Fall/winter 1945-46*

Best seller furs at popular Sears prices. Practical favorites for all around wear, tuxedo style… in dyed opossum, mouton lamb, and Persian paw. $130-160. [$60-80] *Fall/winter 1945-46*

Grand for the games… the fur-like, deep pile is pure wool. Young, casual, warm, teddy bear coats with huge cuffs, cardigan neck. Box coat is fully lined, available in grayish brown or dark brown. Cardigan coat has giant cuffs, warm and cozy on the coldest day. Fully lined, available in grayish brown and dark brown. $25. [$30-50] *Fall/winter 1945-46*

Precious Persian lamb, lustrous jet black, tight curled. A wonder for wear, styled by Sears in front-page fashions… smart for seasons to come. Wide sleeve tuxedo with clever cardigan neckline and saddle shoulders. Rayon lined. Easy drape tuxedo with new balloon sleeves, only superb Hollander-dyed Featherlite Persian details so magnificently. Converts to closed collarless swagger. $407. [$60-80] *Fall/winter 1945-46*

All wool suede soft-line coats in graceful feminine styles, perfect over pretty dresses, or dressmaker suits carry the Kerrybrooke label. Medium gray, medium blue, medium green. $30. [$30-40] *Fall/winter 1945-46*

Shoes & Accessories

Sturdy welt oxfords at thrifty prices. Styles include suede with alligator grain trim, classic blucher with leather sole, alligator grain with rubber sole. Each $2-3. [$20-30] *Fall/winter 1943-44*

Moc-type oxfords – old favorites and new styles. Styles include economy or full priced ghillie ties, or supple suede bluchers, $3-6. [$20-30] *Fall/winter 1943-44*

Change your pumps to suit your costume! Your choice of three qualities in this versatile Sears pump. Good, better, and best quality, available in suede or patent leather. $3-7. [$25-35] *Fall/winter 1943-44*

Get the styles you want and the service you want at a price that you'll like with Action-aires, proven sports favorites. Bluchers, moc-style, and espadrille styles. $3. [$20-30] *Fall/winter 1943-44*

Specially designed oxfords and ghillies for working feet. Steel and plastic-reinforced safety toe models available. $3-7. [$20-30] *Fall/winter 1943-44*

Deluxe Kerrybrooke fur felt hats, add distinction to your ensemble. Bonnets, sailor style, berets, each glamorous and charming. Grosgrain bands with bows or streamers. $5-8. [$10-20] *Fall/winter 1943-44*

Breton Sailor $7.49   Charming Bonnet $5.95   Smart Suit Hat $6.95

C   Popular Padre Sailor $1.98   F   Wool Felt $2.29   Fur Felt $3.98

B   Smart tailored style $2.39   E   Wool Felt $2.39   Fur Felt $3.98

The best known casual hats in America, these wool felt and fur felt give comfort and warmth, and of course a flair for style. $2-4. [$10-20] *Fall/winter 1943-44*

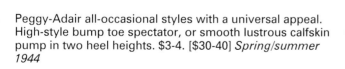

Peggy-Adair all-occasional styles with a universal appeal. High-style bump toe spectator, or smooth lustrous calfskin pump in two heel heights. $3-4. [$30-40] *Spring/summer 1944*

Not rationed! Colorful "spring tonic" footwear. Specially treated Endura-flex soles, guaranteed to give service equal to leather. $2-4. [$10-20] *Spring/summer 1944*

Some bright answers to your ration stamp problem. $3-6. [$30-40] *Spring/summer 1944*

Hand-lasted D'Orsay pump in genuine reptile leather. Army russet alligator leather, or gray ringtail lizard. $10. "Baby doll" anklet to make you look your petite loveliest. Black patent, white suede, or Army russet calfskin. $7. [$30-40] *Spring/summer 1944*

These lovely styles have that coveted "custom" look. Palizzio's open shank, high heel anklet, hand lasted open toe pump give new heights of smartness. $6-9. [$25-35] *Spring/summer 1944*

Colorful Carefrees. Made with Sears flexible wooden soles, guaranteed to give satisfactory wear. Red, white, green, canary yellow, wheat, blue. $3-4. [$10-20] *Spring/summer 1944*

More colorful Carefree Casuals, free and easy, gay and breezy. $2-4. [$10-20] *Spring/summer 1944*

Actionaire fashion hits… gay, youthful leather moc slip-ons. Perfect companions for skirts and anklets, comfortable and well built, made for lots of action. $3. [$10-20] *Spring/summer 1944*

Take a tip from a schoolgirl's notebook. Dawn-to-dark Deb style Mary Jane pump with tailored bow. Anklet style, a footnote that amounts to a forecast. $3-5. [$10-20] *Spring/summer 1944*

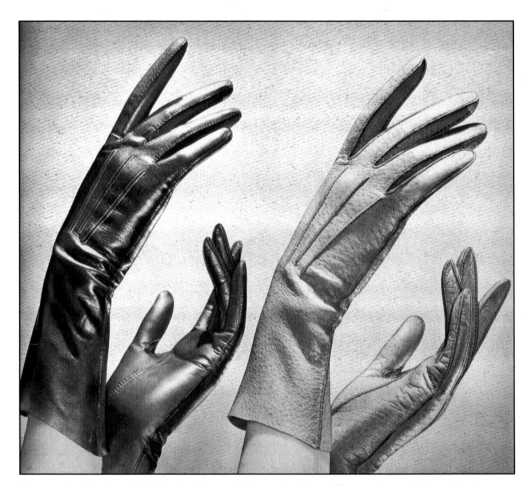

Charmode "topnotcher" classic slip-ons in finest leathers. Glace cabretta (sheep) leather, molds gracefully to your hands. Slim-fingered elegance. Genuine imported Peccary pigskins, rugged and long–wearing. $3-4. [$10-20] *Spring/summer 1944*

No ration stamp required for these smart desk-to-date styles. "Baby doll" ankle strap in a premiere appearance, D'Orsay pump is thrillingly beautiful, truly outstanding complete with a pleated circle bow. $3-4. [$30-40] *Spring/summer 1944*

Colorful fabric bags that add spice to your wardrobe. Practical and roomy, they are grand for sportswear and shopping, but handsome enough to wear with your newest dress-up ensemble. $4 each. [$25-35] *Spring/summer 1944*

Splendid selection of bags in fabrics and leather chosen for their rich good looks and long, sturdy wear. Styled with fine details that include Lucite trim, favorite zipper inside or outside closings. $4 each. Some styles available with gold color plastic initials attached. 20¢ each initial, 50¢ for three. [25-35] *Spring/summer 1944*

Ration-free colorful styles to give your wardrobe a lift. Endura-flex soles, open toe, selected styles open back. $3-4. [$15-25] *Fall/winter 1944-45*

Charmode "Match-Mates" hat and bag sets. Choose the clever beret or the smart calot. Famous buckle back assures better fit and easy adjustability to change the size if you change your hairdo. $5. [$15-25] *Spring/summer 1944*

Mexican-type Play Boys in rich fall colors. Wear them proudly at home, for shopping, at the movies… any indoor or outdoor occasion. Comfortable wedge heels. $3-4. [$15-25] *Fall/winter 1944-45*

Top left:
Women's warm felt and leather slippers… no ration stamp needed. Styles come in wine, rose, blue, brown, and black. $1-2. [$5-15] *Fall/winter 1944-45*

Left:
Actionaires in alligator-grained cowhide. Enduring rationed footwear, built to last. Graceful slip-on style is a foot charmer that spells youth and gaiety. Gives a slender look to legs and ankles. Easy fitting blucher oxford has a low heel for getting places in comfort. $2-6. [$30-40] *Fall/winter 1944-45*

Above:
Actionaire slip-on classics in smartly tailored styles. Favorite "Norwegian" moc-style, designed for the quick tempo and fast gait of modern living. Richly antiqued, the finish glows with many polishings. Low heel with rubber lift. Leather sole slip-on is a four season favorite that has everything in style and comfort. The flat seam moc-type slip-on is poised for action. A perfect teammate for skirts and sweaters, and tailored casuals. All in brown leather only. $3-4. [$20-30] *Fall/winter 1944-45*

Genuine reptile shoes with a foot flattering custom-made look... use your ration stamp today! Black or brown patent. $8-11. [$15-25] *Fall/winter 1944-45*

Not Rationed
L $6.95

Not Rationed
M $2.98

Actionaire sturdy sports styles. Leather storm boot lined with lamb's wool, brown moc-style oxford, classic camp "moc," perennial "bike" oxford, low priced saddle oxford styles. $2-7. [$10-20] *Fall/winter 1944-45*

Favorite moc-type oxfords in 3 qualities. Good, better, best, in antiqued brown, white pigskin, or black leather. $3-6. [$10-20] *Fall/winter 1944-45*

Nurses' type comfort oxford. Loved "best friend" of active women on their feet all day. Roomy last allows perfect foot freedom. A comfort investment for your ration stamp. Black kid or white leather, $2 a pair. [$15-20] *Fall/winter 1944-45*

"Match-mates" hat and bag sets. Head hugger or looped pompadour with drawstring bags to match, in navy blue, black, dark brown, or turf tan. Platter beret or off-the-face bonnet with matching bag in dark brown, back, Kelly green, or bright red. $5.50. [$15-20] *Fall/winter 1944-45*

Kerrybrooke casual hats for all occasions. Fine quality wool or fur felt cloche style hats with long lived smartness and tailored distinction. $2. [$5-15] *Fall/winter 1944-45*

The newest, brightest, and gayest of the 1944 millinery style hats are available for juniors. Pillbox, chelton beret, and tam styles, with matching handbags. $3. [$5-15] *Fall/winter 1944-45*

Charmode women's hats, ageless distinction and youthful flattery. Wool felt – lightweight, luxurious quality and texture. Casablanca sailor, tricorne beret with misty rayon veil, and ruffled edge sailor styles. $4. [$15-25] *Fall/winter 1944-45*

New accessories that add to every outfit. Wool fringed headkerchief in red or copen blue with white. Lacy all wool fascinator, flattery for any age. Delicately feminine, can be worn in three fashions– head shawl, scarf, or turban, in white, copen blue, pink or red. Felt vest and Dutch cap with brightly embroidered snowflakes, in white or red. $1-4. [$5-10] *Fall/winter 1944-45*

A Feather Face-Framer . . . . $3.69 B Sophisticated Pillbox . . . . . $2.49 C Winged Feather Flatterer $3.98 D Bare-brow Feather Flowers $3.9

E The "Banana" Hat . . . . . . $2.79 F Side-pleat Half-Hat . . . . . $2.69 G Head-hugging Matador . . $2.79 H The Dressmaker Drape $1.9

J Ruffled Pomp-adorable . . . $2.79 K Nailhead Coolie Beret . . . . $1.98 L Pompadour Half-Hat . . . . . $1.69 M Bejeweled Rayon Velvet . $2.98

Colorful, stylish hats for all occasions give the 1944 woman a modern, smart look. $2-4. [$15-25] *Fall/winter 1944-45*

Women's work gloves for home, garden, or factory. $1. [$2-5] *Fall/winter 1944-45*

Glamour teams – hat and bag sets to accent your ensemble. Calot and feed bag, Persian lamb-effect cloth on muff bag and wool felt hat, pillbox with matching bellows bag, and bow-back bonnet with matching tulip-top bag in bright colors. $5-8. [$15-25] *Fall/winter 1944-45*

Better handbags in leather and fabric. Fan shape, appreciate the rich, suede-like texture of 100% virgin wool broadcloth. Box bottom pouch is a dress bag that's roomy and beautifully made with a carved frame. Felt disc, outlined in bold white saddle stitching. Throw it over-the-shoulder for a casual or dressy feel. $6. [$15-25] *Fall/winter 1944-45*

Handbags that you wear season after season – in artificial leather, felt, or real cape leather. Most are rayon lined, fitted with coin cases, mirrors, and handy snap fasteners. $2 each. [$15-25] *Fall/winter 1944-45*

Happy-go-lucky play shoes, gaily youthful. Cheerful accessories for spring and summer wardrobes in comfortable, romantic styles and bright bird colors. $2-3. [$10-20] *Spring/summer 1945*

Luxury bags in genuine corde. Now you can enjoy the thrill of owning a really elegant handbag, moderately priced from Sears. Graceful, undated styles with the bold touch of gleaming lucite. Black and brown. $12. [$15-25] *Fall/winter 1944-45*

Free-n-easy playtimers. Back again! Colorful, genuine leathers you've been waiting for. Sparkling nailheads, scallops, feather-flight glove flexible cork platforms and innersoles provide joyous comfort and style. Send ration stamp. $3-4. [$] *Spring/summer 1945*

Youthful "Honor Roll" debs, informally casual or frivolously feminine. Favorites adored by the sweater 'n skirt set. Sandals, slip-ons, wedgies, and pumps. $3-6. [$20-30] *Spring/summer 1945*

Nurse-type oxfords are trim, comfortable shoes for active, day-long wear. $4-6. [$20-30] *Spring/summer 1945*

Flexible pillow-soft cushions help reduce foot fatigue. Square toe ghillie, five-eyelet kid tie, two-eyelet calf tie styles available. $4. [$20-30] *Spring/summer 1945*

Exquisite "Punchinellos," temptingly different and as new as tomorrow. Punched out, scalloped, provocatively feminine. $3-4. [$20-30] *Spring/summer 1945*

Five-Eyelet Tie, $6.45   "Suit-able" Pump, $6.45   Graceful Step-in, $6.45   Sandal Beauty, $6.45

Tailored beauties, keyed to the new mood of graceful elegance. Sparkling genuine reptile skins, young shoe fashions have lasting beauty. $6-11. [$20-30] *Spring/summer 1945*

The Heroine Hat $1.98   The Rough-Straw Cartwheel $2.98   The Twin-Bow Sailor $2.98

The Sweetheart Pump $1.98   The Gardenia Bonnet $2.98   The Coolie Hat $3.69

Glamorous brims, face flatterers for summer-time wear. Popular hats with big-sweep brims, youthfully detailed, face-framers. $2-4. [$20-30] *Spring/ summer 1945*

The J-Ring Calot $4.98   The Off-Side Cap $4.98   The Baby Helmet $2.98

The Crown-Clinging Hat $1.98   The Gardenia Hat $2.98   The Hyacinth Hat $2.98

Little flowered hats: J-ring calot, off-side cap, baby helmet, crown-clinging hat, gardenia, hyacinth, all-flower, young calot, and nosegay hats for that soft feminine look. $2-5. [$5-15] *Spring/summer 1945*

Carefree gypsy style shoes, sparkling confetti colors and only the newest, freshest styles. Pretty play shoes make great vacation companions! $2-3. [$5-15] *Spring/summer 1945*

| E ADORABLE FLATTIE ...... $1.94 | G CANDY STRIPES ...... $2.98 |
| B GAY SLIP-ON ...... $3.29 | J TRIM TAILORED TIE ...... $3.29 |

Thrifty artificial leather box bags, envelope bags, and shoulder straps. Black, navy blue, brown, selected styles in bright red. $2-4. [$10-20] *Spring/summer 1945*

| B COLLAR BOX BAG .... $2.29 | C VANITY BOX BAG .... $3.49 | D BAR BOX BAG .... $3.49 |
| F TRIANGLE FLAP BAG .... $2.29 | | G FITTED BAG .... $3.49 |

| B THE 4-LOOP CALOT $1.98 | C THE POSY PILLBOX $1.98 | D THE CUT-OUT BEANIE $1.98 |
| F THE BEAU CATCHER HAT $1.69 | G THE DUTCHIE $1.98 | H THE LEAF PILLBOX $2.98 |

Sears Merricaps, new fashions for the young set. 4-loop calot, posy pillbox, cut-out beanie, beau catcher with veil, dutchie with veil, leaf pillbox, snug-fit calot, swing cloche, and miniature beret with feathers pulled through. $2-3. [$5-15] *Spring/summer 1945*

Ⓛ Open Toe. Bare Back. 2-inch Heel. $4.25 and $6.95   Bows not included in prices shown   Ⓜ Open Toe. Bare Back. 2½-inch Heel. $4.25 and $6.95

Peggy Adair pumps, simple and smart for that well groomed look. Made fashionably feminine with bows. Open toe bare back with two or two-and-a-half inch heels, in black patent or white suede leather. Open toe closed back, same heights, same colors. $4-7. [$30-40] *Spring/summer 1945*

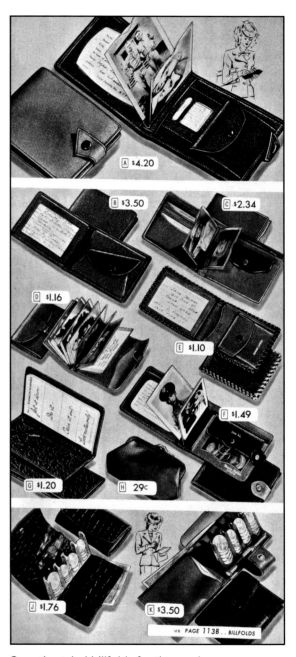

Ⓐ $4.20
Ⓑ $3.50
Ⓒ $2.34
Ⓓ $1.16
Ⓔ $1.10
Ⓕ $1.49
Ⓖ $1.20
Ⓗ 29c
Ⓙ $1.76
Ⓚ $3.50
PAGE 113B .. BILLFOLDS

Smartly styled billfolds for the modern woman. Federal excise tax included. $2-5. [$5-15] *Spring/summer 1945*

Ration-free date n' party pickups for fun-loving feet. $4-5. [$10-20] *Fall/winter 1945-46*

Popular, casual wedgie style make walking a joy. Easy-bending, soft cork platforms and innersoles. Moc-type, platform tie, spectator slip-on styles available in brown, brown crushed leather, and black. $4. [$30-40] *Fall/winter 1945-46*

Kerrybrooke felts for every outfit. Laced casual, corded brim, rainbow casual, platform beret with veil, platter brim, and tambourine berets with veils, shirred puff, forward bumper, dress-up bumper. $2-3. [$15-25] *Fall/winter 1945-46*

| B LACED CASUAL $1.98 | C CORDED BRIM $1.98 | D RAINBOW CASUAL $2.49 |
| E PLATFORM BERET $2.98 | F PLATTER BRIM $2.98 | H TAMBOURINE BERET $3.98 |

Top-fashion platform wedgies for ease-afoot. Gleaming nail heads to step up your costume sparkle. Fun-time band sandal, five eyelet U-throated tie in pretty cotton gabardine, fashion bow sling back, and slip on styles. $3-6. [$10-20] *Fall/winter 1945-46*

Gay, little stay-at-homes softie slippers. Fur-trimmed, embroidered, and rayon satin trimmed styles, made for comfort in your leisure hours. $2. [$5-10] *Fall/winter 1945-46*

Teen Girls' Fashions

Dresses

Popular junior dresses, to wear from coke-time to curfew-time! Corduroy, crepe, cotton styles. $5-7. [$10-20] *Fall/winter 1943-44*

A—Peg pocketed sailor $3.98
B—Dirndl-effect dater $4.98
C—Button-front coat dress $3.98

Juniors everyday favorites in solid color rayons. White braid on collar gives ship-shape in medium blue or red. Red and white candy stripes sweeten up square neckline, full front, and back gored skirt. Cluster front tucks, shirred front skirt. Charmette's rayon crepe in Cadet blue, gold, and rosewood. Velveray design, dirndl skirt of form fitting basque dress. Back buttoned in soldier blue and medium green. Red pom-pom and fringe add gay note to figure flattering tie-back princess dress. Gray or medium blue with red trim. $3-5. [$5-15] *Fall/winter 1943-44*

Classic simplicity and all-time wearability team up with the clean-cut smartness juniors want. Streamlined rayon Macomba cloth fly front dress buttons from waist. Front full skirt has easy swing and double-buckled self belt. Red and aqua blue. $8. [$5-15] *Fall/winter 1943-44*

A-Checked Chesterfield dress $2.98   B-Border print dirndl $2.98   C-Ruffled plaid jumper $1.98

Juniors' Luxables in cotton and rayon. Checked chesterfield, border print dirndl, self ruffled jumper, embroidered pique, and Organdy flower trimmed styles are nicely detailed and refreshingly colorful. $2-4. [$5-15] *Fall/winter 1943-44*

Mallinson's new rayon Cruisaline dresses. Surplice front dress, contour closure. Button front dress, tie front, set-in belt. Colors: Contrast bordered blossom blue, blossom pink, blossom green. $9. [$5-15] *Spring/summer 1944*

Skirts and blouses…
in gay peasant styles
and colors. $2-4. [$5-
15] *Spring/summer
1944*

Peg-Pocketed Dirndl. $1.98   Eyelet-Edged Dirndl. $3.98   Ruffly "U" Neck Dirndl. $3.98

Cool cotton sheers for
juniors. Favorites for dating
or dancing. $2-4. [$5-15]
Spring/summer 1944

Cotton brunch coats.
Cool, washable for
work or leisure.
Button front and
wrap around styles in
dirndl and seer-
sucker. Assorted
colorful floral
designs. $2-3. [$5-15]
Spring/summer 1944

Rayon-and-cotton
favorites in misses
sizes. Button front,
basque dirndl,
surplice fly front, and
classic fly front styles
in rich fall colors. $4
each. [$5-15] *Fall/
winter 1944-45*

Juniors' rayons… date-raters and work-wonders. Perfect for on the job or on the town. Newest styles compliment and flatter any figure. $5-6. [$5-15] *Spring/summer 1945*

Casual Separates and Sportswear

Suits to wear alone in fall and spring, or under coats all winter. In colorful checks and plaids with padded shoulders, interlined lapels and 2 inch hems, these Shetland-type part wool skirts, jackets and cardigans are a grand value at Sears low prices. $6-10. [$5-15] *Fall/winter 1943-44*

Casual, carefree jumpers and suits, styled in a lively new way. V-top all wool in striking hound's-tooth. Jerkin suit with carefree tomboy look, tailored in soft gray menswear flannel, blazer suit with cardigan jacket piped in checks, and all wool bow-tie suit in wonderful soft textured hound's-tooth checks. $6-14. [$5-15] *Fall/winter 1945-46*

From Lake Placid to Sun Valley, you won't find a smarter sweater than the boxy prairie pullover. Made of warm wool and cotton, it has a cowboy motif on the front. $3. The Norwegian type cardigan is pretty all over with an adorable squirrel motif, in a becoming fitted style. $4. A suede front cardigan is tremendously popular with well dressed women. The front panel is fine quality suede leather that's as soft as Chamois. $6. [$20-30] *Fall/winter 1943-44*

Color-spice your wardrobe with several of these gay, bright sweaters. The dressy two-tone pullover and the smart longer length pullover are delightfully soft and knit with the finest wool, rayon, and yarns. The short sleeve crew neck Midgie cardigan is fashioned in an attractive knit-and-purl stitch that gives lovely lines, with rib knit saddle shoulders for a military air. $2. [$5-15] *Fall/ winter 1943-44*

Kerrybrooke man-tailored slacks are a Sears famous specialty. In styles like herringbone tweed, pin-wale cotton corduroy, Parker Wilder tweed, and spun rayon and "aralac" have a back vent for simplest altering, and a waistband lined to hug the waist and keep your shirt tucked in. $3-4. [$5-15] *Fall/winter 1943-44*

Champion corduroy button front sports dress, pin-wale ribbed, extra warm. Figure-wise pleats at waistline, and a skirt with plenty of swing. Wonderful colors: spruce green, brown, or navy. The button front jumper in finely ribbed corduroy comes in red, brown, or navy, and it's character changes with a change of blouse, tailored classics by day, frilly feminine by night. $5-6 [$10-20] *Fall/winter 1943-44*

You go to work or play in washable cotton slack suits. You just can't beat them for durability, washability, coolness, comfort, and low price. Cotton seersucker in blue and white or green and white, sanforized cotton denim in medium blue, and woven striped chambray in white with red or blue. $3-4. [$30-50] *Spring/summer 1944*

Polo shirts… classics in knit cottons, rayon-and-cotton. From Dallas to Duluth, from Boston to Beverly Hills, polo shirts are first choice for all around sports wear. $1-2. [$5-15] *Spring/summer 1944*

June O'Day all wool classics. Cardigans and pullovers to top your skirts and slacks, in bright, springy colors. $2-4. [$15-25] *Spring/ summer 1944*

Ⓐ PRINTED SEERSUCKER........$1.98   Ⓑ PERCALE TWO PIECE........$1.98   Ⓒ OXFORD CLOTH DIRNDL........$1.98

Washable cottons in teen sizes. Thrifty percales… stripes, solids, and checks. $2. [$5-15] *Spring/ summer 1944*

The daisy polka dotted rayon jumper, in powder blue, red, green, each with white velveray-applied polka dots. $3. [$5-15] *Spring/ summer 1944*

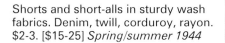

Shorts and short-alls in sturdy wash fabrics. Denim, twill, corduroy, rayon. $2-3. [$15-25] *Spring/summer 1944*

Sea-Ho Swim suits… flattering, action cut styles. They're gay, colorful young suits. Jacquard bengaline (rayon and cotton) in a pert and pretty open midriff suit. In French blue and yellow. Velva-sheen slender princess style suit with daisy chain appliqué, in royal blue and black. Cotton seersucker dressmaker suit in red print or blue. $3-4. [$30-50] *Spring/summer 1944*

Colorful casual slack suits in crown-tested Veranna rayon. California-inspired styles, fine tailoring. $5-6. [$25-35] *Spring/summer 1944*

Light-weight slacks… perfect for work and play. $2-4. [$5-15] *Spring/summer 1944*

Teen's classic three button sport suit, pacific 100% wool Shetland-type tweed in bright red, copen blue, or sun gold. $10. [$10-20] *Spring/ summer 1944*

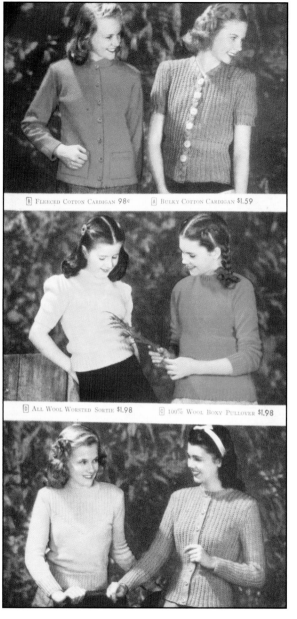

B FLEECED COTTON CARDIGAN 98¢   A BULKY COTTON CARDIGAN $1.59

D ALL WOOL WORSTED SORTIE $1.98   C 100% WOOL BOXY PULLOVER $1.98

June O'Day Jr. trademarked schoolgirls' sweaters in cardigan, pullover, and coat styles to team with skirts and slacks and give her lots of changes. Young America adores them for smartness, comfort, and beauty. $2-3. [$15-25] *Fall/winter 1944-45*

A PULLOVER $2.50   B CARDIGAN $2.89

June O'Day all wool fine gauge classics. Quality tailored into every detail. Long boxy pullover or cardigan, both available in three wool qualities. $2-5. [$15-25] *Fall/winter 1944-45*

Juniors' Botany virgin wool flannel scalloped dress has a smooth fit. Dressy enough to do a quick-change act from desk to date. Belt, set in at back, ties in front. Violet and aqua. $10. [$5-15] *Fall/winter 1944-45*

Finely tailored skirts in all or part wool. Color takes the lead, both in striking solo shades and in the youthful harmony of plaids. Block or clan-type plaids available. $3-6. [$5-15] *Fall/winter 1944-45*

Sears is known for fine, low priced riding wear. Prairie pants, jodhpurs, and saddle pants offer a precise fit and long wear. $3-5. [$5-20] *Fall/winter1944-45*

Kerrybrooke cotton shirtfrock in famous Lonsdale cord, a fine corded chambray with stripes woven in. Pleats on front bodice and skirt, back gores, and roomy pockets. Colors: copen-and-white, red-and-white, brown-and-white, green-and-white, lavender-and-white. $4. [$5-15] *Fall/winter 1944-45*

Sports separates in smart menswear gay. Jumpers, trousers, skirts, and jackets, each expertly tailored for the active junior. $2-6. [$5-15] *Spring/summer 1945*

103

Top-fashion Sea-Ho swim suits are youthful and daring, in rayon taffeta 2-piece, satin-like rayon 1 piece, and print 'n' plain half-skirt style rayon jersey with velva-sheen back. Knit cotton lining throughout. $3-4. [$30-50] *Spring/ summer 1945*

Outdoor sports clothes especially designed for golf, styled for comfort. Tops in white, skirts in dark brown, dark green, or red. $3-6. [$5-15] *Spring/ summer 1945*

Sears best junior rayons make you look your best. Multi-button 2-piece suit dress, ruffled U-neck dress, draped torso, and side-buttoned dressy pastel dress. $7-9. [$5-15] *Spring/summer 1945*

A YELLOW LEATHER JACKET $15.95

Popular riding jackets in your favorite new styles. Yellow leather jacket, made like an officer's field jacket. Hugs figure closely, resists wind and weather, always looks trim and neat. 100% virgin wool tweed riding jacket, smart brown and gray mixture. Smart women love the wide slimming waistband, fine tailoring. The western jacket, top-flight sports favorite worn by movie stars and smart girls everywhere. Flattering, jaunty, and comfortable. In soft suede leather with self-leather fringe trim on front, back yoke, and sleeve like a real cowboy. Expertly tailored. $12-16. [$30-75] *Spring/summer 1945*.

A $1.59 $2.07 Pullover Cardigan   C $1.98   E $2.56

Bright mixers for the sweater-loving school crowd. Gay colors in muffin-warm all wool. Cardigans, boxy pullovers, Honeylane virgin worsted classics. Colors: navy, bright red, dark green, copen blue. $2-4. [$15-25] *Fall/winter 1945-46*

Sleepwear

Butcher-boy style Jamarettes. Sturdy percale. Drawstring roomy trousers and full boxy top. Rose check and copen blue check. Sanforized cotton broadcloth in wine multi-stripes or blue multi-stripes. Rayon French crepe in rose or light blue. $2-4. [$5-15] *Spring/summer 1944*

Co-ed elastic knit cross-wise stretch girdles and panties, designed for lightweight control and stretch-with-your-figure freedom. Girdles for everyday, general wear, and panties for active wear with slacks or when you go out without stockings. Available in nude (pale flesh pink) color. $2-4. [$5-10] *Fall/winter 1945-46*

Quilted robes for rich warmth. Solid color rayon poplin dirndl-effect robe is young and perky with figure-hugging bodice. Red with white lining, green with white lining, and navy with red lining, all available. Printed checked rayon robe with the smart Chesterfield look, complete with rayon velvet notched collar. $9-14. [$5-15] *Fall/winter 1944-45*

Outerwear

Teen classics, the famous coats all young America wants. Boy coat, Hollywood wrap coat, and fly-front Chesterfield styles in strong, bright colors. $14. [$10-20] *Fall/winter 1943-44*

Coats for rainy days or fair weather. Reversible boy coat in solid red or soldier blue, or in pastel blue and pastel rose plaid. Boy raincoat in cotton gabardine, natural tan only. Military raincape in red or blue, and classic Navy reefer. $2-9. [$5-15] *Spring/summer 1944*

Wind and weather-resistant snow suits, fully lined with warm, fleecy cotton Kasha. Cotton poplin jacket, double breasted all wool suit with Laskinlamb fur collar, two-tone all wool snow-suit with clever evergreen appliqué, and neatly belted warm wool jacket, well-tailored and fitted. $6-14. [$5-15] *Fall/winter 1943-44*.

Coat classics styled for teens. Classic boy coat, officers coat, wrap-tie, and Chesterfield styles. Can be worn year round for any occasion. $9-11. [$10-20] *Spring/summer 1944*

Teen classic suits and double duty sets, coats with matching snow pants. Cozy warmth plus plenty of style – a coat to wear for school or Sunday best. Fun, fashionable styles at reasonable prices. $9-15. [$5-15] *Fall/winter 1944-45*

Girls' active sportswear, rich textured corduroy slacks, and jumpers. Gray part wool flannels, in man-tailored styles. $2-4. [$5-15] *Fall/winter 1944-45*

The western jacket and the boxy topper in suede leather. Two top-flight favorites, smart because they're jaunty and young-looking, popular because they go nicely over everything. Boxy topper in leaf green, nut brown, and chamois. The western jacket, frontier-type fringe that's worn by movie stars, in camel tan and nut brown. $16-20. [$50-75] *Fall/winter 1944-45*

THE TWIN-BUTTON CHESTERFIELD shown in gold, $14.98 and $19.98. Also comes in mint (med. green), cocoa (med. brown), lt. soft blue, below

CLASSIC BOY COAT shown in mint (med. green), $14.98 and $19.98. Also comes in gold, cocoa (medium brown), light soft blue, below

MARK 5 PAGE 77 . . . . COATS

When does a coat have everything in its favor? When it's a Kerrybrooke. Color-bright coats in soft monotone wool. $15-20. [$25-35] *Spring/summer 1945*

Grand for the games… the fur-like, deep pile is pure wool. Young, casual, warm, teddy bear coats with huge cuffs, cardigan neck. Box coat is fully lined, in grayish brown or dark brown. Cardigan coat has giant cuffs, warm and cozy on the coldest day. Fully lined, in grayish brown and dark brown. $25. [$30-50] *Fall/winter 1945-46*

B HEART SHAPED BONNET $1.98   C BOW CLOCHE $2.98   D DUTCH TREAT $2.98

F POMPADOUR RUFFLE $1.98   G CORDE-LIKE CALOT $2.98   H JEWEL STUDDED CALOT $2.98

Hats smartly keyed to your clothes, for frilly, feminine fashions. Match them with dramatic, date-time dresses, or tailored togs and classic clothes. $2-4. [$10-20] *Fall/winter 1945-46*

Men's Fashions

Suits and Dress Wear

The season's newest fabrics, Fashion Tailored dress slacks of virgin wool and rayon worsted. Colorful, neat stripes, conservative tailoring. Medium brown, gray, or blue. Lively handsome overplaid, sturdy hard finished, youthful styling. $6.45. [$5-15] *Fall/winter 1943-44*

Finest suits… 100% virgin wool worsted fabric. Super tailoring. Overplaid with fabric distinction in blue, brown, or gray. Dignified stripes in regular or stout sizes, 6 button vest, well tailored trousers. Available in gray stripe or blue stripe. $27.50 each. [$5-15] *Spring/summer 1944*

Fashion Tailored novelty checked wool sportscoat and superb lustrous gabardine slacks, in tan or blue. $25 for entire ensemble. [$5-15] *Spring/summer 1944*

Heavyweight virgin wool worsted suits, excellent workmanship. Fashion Tailored label for a perfect fit. $25. [$5-15] *Fall/winter 1944-45*

Deluxe Fashion Tailored means your suit will compare with the finest, superbly tailored perfect fitting suit, deluxe in every respect. Handsome chalk stripes, double breasted, and Glen plaid, single or double breasted. $27. [$5-15] *Fall/winter 1944-45*

Pacemaker sanforized matched work outfits, neat, strong, and comfortable. Vat dyed shantung-effect cool cotton poplin, long wearing herringbone drills and jeans, and sunfast medium weight sturdy cotton twill. Perfect summer weight to keep you cool and crisp looking. Available in a wide choice of practical, attractive colors. $1- 3. [$5-15] *Spring/summer 1945*

Boys' Sturdy Slacks
Neat, long-wearing fabrics for work or dress

Cool, easy-to-care-for summer trousers… the right style and weight for work, sports, or dress. Cotton and rayon gabardine, poplin, and combed cotton blends, these firmly woven pants come in blue, brown, Army tan, blue with white stripes, and tan with brown stripes. $2-3. [$5-15] *Spring/summer 1945*

Right:
Fashion Tailored virgin wool worsted suits, excellent quality. $25. [$5-15] *Spring/summer 1945*

Far right:
Royalton thrifty dress shirts. Full cut cotton percales. $1-2. [$5-15] *Spring/summer 1945*

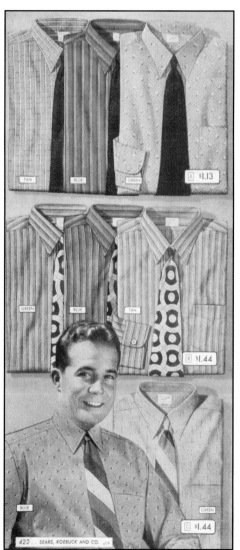

Service Work Clothes

Hercules brand drum major overalls, long wearing and extra roomy. Striped or blue high back denim overalls, and coats to match. $1.50 each. [$40-50] *Spring/summer 1944*

Contrasting slack suits for summer comfort. Cool rayon, rayon gabardine, and lightweight tropical weave style slacks, shirts have convertible collars and come in various solids and plaids. Each outfit: $11-15. [$5-15] *Spring/summer 1944*

Nation-alls… sanforized for a lasting perfect fit. Your choice of covert or hickory stripe, or aviation style work wear. Designed for comfort and to last. $2-3. [$40-50] *Spring/summer 1944*

Sturdy oak knit shirts, all combed cotton with interlocking stitches. Heavy, stretchy fabric for comfort, with extra long sleeves to protect your arms. Available in navy blue, brown or tan. Factory shirts for industrial work, pre-shrunk cotton gabardine, efficiency styled. Wear it in or out of your trousers, and the two-way collar looks equally good with or without a tie. Tan or blue. $2. [$5-15] *Spring/summer 1944*

Casual Sportswear

Royal Ascot famous dress shirts, sanforized cotton broadcloths, noted for weight and wear. Patterns woven-through. [$5-15] *Spring/summer 1944*

Fashion Tailored sports coats, 100% virgin wool, herringbone tweed pattern or smartess glen plaid. Coats are half lined, sleeves fully lined with fine quality Earl-Glo rayon. $13-15. Wool worsted Bedford cord slacks, woven into fine gabardine with a smart raised rib. Gabardine slacks woven in fine herringbone weave. $7.45-7.75. 2-piece coat and slacks outfit, at savings, $20-23. [$5-15] *Fall/winter 1943-44*

Pilgrim Nobility year-around sports shirts. Teca and rayon printed patterns, medium long point collars with two flap pockets. Woven with 2-ply rayon that has two threads in each strand of yarn instead of one for extra body. $3-5. [$5-10] *Fall/winter 1943-44*

Fashion tailored dress trousers, excellent in quality and value. Stylish glen plaids, neat pencil stripes, blended worsted overplaid, virgin wool worsted. $5-8. [$5-15] *Spring/ summer 1944*

English rib effect sweaters, virgin wool worsted. Exceptionally soft and long wearing. Coat style or pullover styles, camel tan, blue, luggage brown. $5-8. [$5-15] *Spring/summer 1944*

Wool sports coats and smart slacks, Fashion Tailored trademarked. Herringbone twill coat in blue or tan with calvary twill gabardine slacks in blue or brown. Glen plaid coat in brown or blue, with wool worsted gabardine slacks in cocoa brown or blue. $18-23. [$5-15] *Spring/summer 1944*.

Fashion Tailored

Leisure coats in leather and fine fabrics. Two-tone wool and suede leather Leisure coat, chocolate brown front is soft, glove-tanned split suede leather, all wool back, sleeves, and collar are brown plaid tweed. $35. [$40-50] Twill "field-club" sports hat in closely woven tan color cotton twill with smart contrasting brown band. $3. [$5-10] *Spring/summer 1944*

Fashion Tailored all virgin wool leisure coats, unusually designed, and very comfortable. Colorful, novelty check all wool on front, back and lapels with contrasting virgin wool worsted gabardine on sleeves and collars. Colors: tan two-tone, blue two-tone. $15. [$25-35] *Fall/winter 1944-45*

Plain "baby shaker" pullover, 65% zephyr wool mixed with 35% mohair wool, lustrous, rich, and soft. Pullover or coat style English rib effect sweater, in camel tan, luggage tan, or blue. $5-8. [$5-15] *Fall/winter 1944-45*

118

Patterned cotton flannel shirts, heavy-weight, sanforized, husky and full cut in bright patterns. Perfect for all-around wear. $1-2. [$5-15] *Fall/winter 1944-45*

Part or all wool pullover sweaters, alpine design knit in a reindeer motif, or heavyweight virgin wool in plaid argyle pattern. $5-7. [$5-15] *Fall/winter 1944-45*

Year round sports shirts, Nobility brand. Pre-shrunk cotton with plaid front, or two-ply fabric of spun and teca rayon. Solid color or plaid front with plain color back, sleeves, and trim. $3-4. [$5-15] *Fall/winter 1944-45*

Sleeveless pullovers, virgin wool worsted medium or medium heavy weight. Royal Ascot brand, superbly knit, in camel tan. Nobility brand sweater in maroon with white design or camel tan with brown design. $3-4. [$5-10] *Fall/winter 1944-45*

C $2.95

D $3.98

Sports combinations, mix 'em or match 'em, style your own outfit. Distinctively styled sports coat and fine twill gabardine slacks. Two-button herringbone coat, or glen plaid sports coat. Linen and hymo interlinings, handsomely cut through the shoulders. Include twill or wool gabardine slacks for a perfect ensemble. $23. [$5-15] *Fall/winter 1944-45*

Fashion Tailored sportswear, gabardine front loafer coat with youthful dash, and deluxe worsted gabardine 2-piece suits. In two-tone blue or tan. $15-25. [$5-15] *Spring/summer 1945*

Gabardine cotton tee shirt and sanforized white gabardine slacks, just the outfit for active sports! Ideal for tennis and golf, light, comfortable, with the correct style and easy of action. White only. $1-4. [$5-15] *Spring/summer 1945*

Long sleeve sports shirts, "sandgrain" rayon in plain colors, or two tone with pin check front. These soft, lustrous shirts are good in any climate. $3-4. [$5-15] *Spring/summer 1945*

Slack suits in cool, comfortable summer fabrics, available in handsome color combinations. Gabardine slacks with a fine cool rayon plaid shirt, or sanforized poplin slacks with an unusually well tailored shirt to make the man. $5-7. [$5-15] *Spring/summer 1945*

Men's riding wear that sets the pace in style and fit. $5-7. [$5-15] *Spring/summer 1945*

Nobility brand short sleeve sport shirts, soft spun rayon, "austinized" fabric styles in tan plaids, blue plaids, or solid whites, tans, and blues. $2-3. [$5-15] *Spring/summer 1945*

Wool pullovers for men, casual sporty or "dress up" styles. $4-6. [$5-15]
Fall/winter 1945-46

Coat style sweaters, husky and plenty warm. Rolled shawl collar is double knit to hold its shape. Buttons up close to your neck for extra protection and warmth. Medium weight or heavy weight, one for every season. $2-3. [$5-15]
Fall/winter 1945-46

Pilgrim classic sports coat, 100% virgin wool worsted, tightly spun, warm, and durable. Medium weight or heavyweight fabrics. Brown heather, dark gray, navy blue. $4-6. [$5-15] *Fall/winter 1945-46*

Underwear and Sleepwear

Genuine Beacon cotton blanket robes, Pilgrim Kingfield, choice of plaid or soft, ombre pattern. Big thick heavyweights, wrap style. One pocket. $5 each. [$50-75] *Fall/winter 1943-44*

America's No. 1 Robe style, the wrap-around model. Spur rayon gabardine diagonal "ribby" weave, double shawl collar, matching sash. Soft brushed rayon style with sleeves set-in the way your suit coat is made, giving a more perfect fit. $6. [$5-15] *Fall/winter 1943-44*

Slippers are NOT rationed. Everett, opera, rayon plush collar, casual, kidskin uppers, slide fastener, and ankle high styles available. Flexible sewed rubber and leather heels. All available in brown, except ankle high style in black kid. $1-4. [$5-15] *Fall/winter 1943-44*

Combed cotton sateen pajamas, soft and comfortable. Paisley or medium figure patterns, blue and cream color grounds. $4. [$5-15] *Spring/summer 1944*

Pilgrim Kingfield sanforized pajamas, coat or pullover top. Royal Ascot soft cotton, peppermint stripes. $2. [$5-15] *Spring/summer 1944*

Lustrous, cozy rayon robes for bundling up on cold winter nights. $6-15. [$5-15] *Fall/winter 1944-45*

Rib knit cotton union suit, long sleeve or short sleeve ankle length styles available. Cream and white. $1-2. [$5-10] *Fall/winter 1944-45*

Wool and part flannel robes, full length wrap models in blue and maroon. [$5-15] *Fall/winter 1944-45*

Nobility brand flannel robes, 100% virgin wool worsted. Medium, medium heavy, or heavyweight in rich plain colors or soft plaid patterns. $14-20. [$5-15] *Fall/winter 1944-45*

Right:
Shirts and shorts fit snugly under your slacks and suits, soft finish and luster. Full roomy panel seat especially for your comfort. $1. [$2-5] *Fall/winter 1944-45*

Far right:
Stretchy knit wool worsted swim trunks, "drop needle" stitch, Or smart woven "boxer" style swim trunks, in solids or Hawaiian prints. Fabric is stretchy, snuggly, and dries quickly. $2-3. [$25-35] *Spring/ summer 1945*

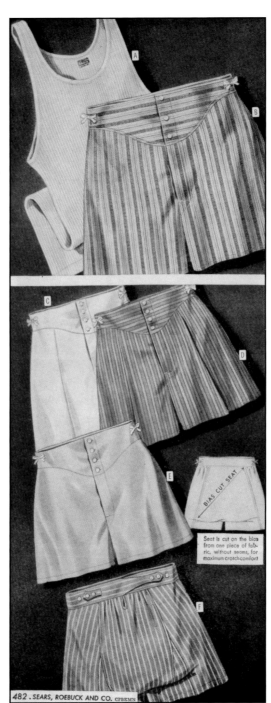

482 . SEARS, ROEBUCK AND CO. CPBEMN

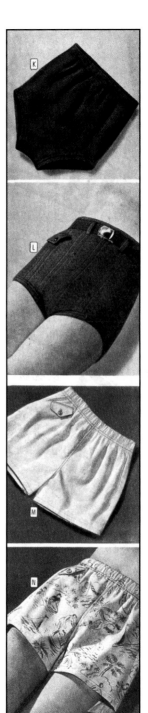

Right:
Knit tee shirts, all short sleeves. Diamond, accordion, ladder, and cable pattern stitches. Perfect for year round wear, fits snugly and comfortably, never binds. $1-2. [$15-25] *Spring/summer 1945*

Far right:
Full length robes, in cotton seersucker, pongee, beacon blanket cloth, wool flannel, or terry cloth. These rugged robes are finely tailored, and especially warm and comfortable on chilly nights. $3-7. [$5-15, $50-75 for seersucker and Beacon] *Spring/summer 1945*

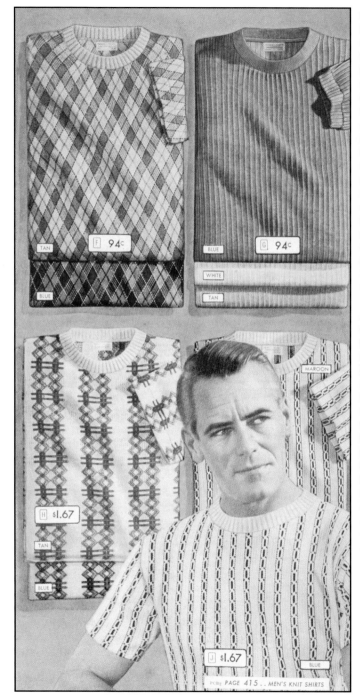

A Woven cotton seersucker......$3.89   B Washable cotton pongee.....$4.88

C Famous Beacon blanket cloth...$5.79   D 50% wool...$6.88

E
Heavyweight
cotton terry cloth
$5.29

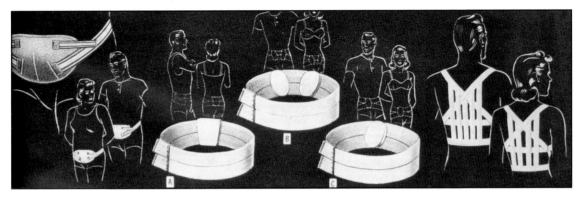

Ritespot supports for men and women, for pendulous abdomen. Helps relieve backaches, protects from hernias, and helps you achieve good posture. $2-4. [$2-5] *Fall/winter 1945-46*

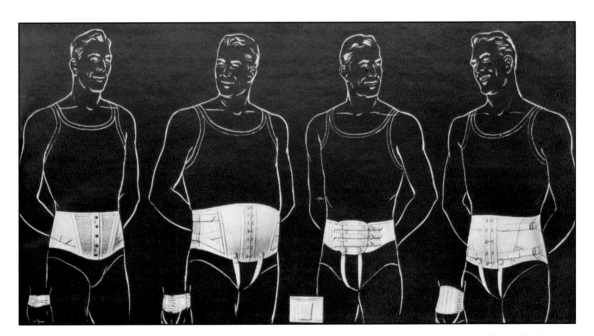

Men's Gale abdominal supports with laces, sacro-iliac and sacro-lumbar support. $3-6. [$2-5] *Fall/winter 1945-46*

Outerwear

"Carefree" leisure coats, 100% virgin wool, two-tone, and glen plaid and calvary twill wool styles. Roomy, fully cut chests and shoulders. Seams are piped with rayon. Deep yoke of rich, lustrous Earl-Glo rayon in each. $8-10. [$40-50] *Fall/winter 1943-44*

Sporty fingertip coats in real capeskin leather and genuine velofleece. Expertly selected leather is warm and windproof. Completely lined with iridescent rayon. Neat fly front, two snappy diagonal pockets. Modern yoke front and back, neat stitching at bottom and cuffs. $19.50. [$50-75] Luxurious velofleece has a fur-like pile which insulates from cold. Beautifully tailored with padded shoulders and interlined collar and lapels that hold their shape. $15. [$15-25] *Fall/winter 1943-44*

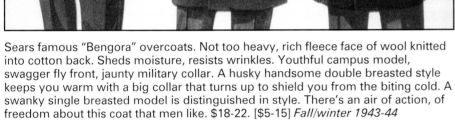

Sears famous "Bengora" overcoats. Not too heavy, rich fleece face of wool knitted into cotton back. Sheds moisture, resists wrinkles. Youthful campus model, swagger fly front, jaunty military collar. A husky handsome double breasted style keeps you warm with a big collar that turns up to shield you from the biting cold. A swanky single breasted model is distinguished in style. There's an air of action, of freedom about this coat that men like. $18-22. [$5-15] *Fall/winter 1943-44*

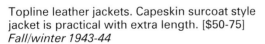

Topline leather jackets. Capeskin surcoat style jacket is practical with extra length. [$50-75] *Fall/winter 1943-44*

Rich, warm all wool Mackinaws. Fully lined all wool plaids, all wool melton, all wool with removable sheepskin lining. Long enough for warmth yet short enough for comfort. $9-17. [$5-15] *Fall/winter 1944-45*

All virgin wool Fashion Tailored leisure coats. "California Clipper" styled in Hollywood with braided trim edges. Solid color front of suede cloth with novelty check wool back, collar, and sleeves. Colors: Tan and blue two-tone. Glen plaid and suede cloth with good looking solid color Park-suede on front and lapels with a colorful glen plaid on sleeves, back, and collar. $9-13. [$40-50] *Fall/winter 1944-45*

Hercules fine quality, smartly styled leather jackets. Regulation Air Force, Aviator's type capeskin, and Cossack style capeskin styles. $11-17. [$50-75] *Fall/winter 1944-45*

Popular overcoat styles in sturdy, warm fabrics. Jaunty "All American" Coacher in richly blended fleece, swagger fly front, military collar (camel tan, medium brown, teal blue), fleecy overplaid double breasted (dark gray, rich blue, beaver brown), and Hollywood styled with swanky long rolling lapels and broad, athletic shoulders. Vigorous and youthful, the sturdy tailoring assures you long wear and perfect fit (dark blue melton). $16-19. [$5-15] *Fall/winter 1944-45*

All wool stag coat and breeches outfit. Warm 33-ounce weight all wool in red and black plaid, moisture repellent. Double fabric over shoulders, back, and knees. Laced bottom breeches. Coat: $8. Breeches: $6. [$5-15] *Fall/winter 1944-45*

Warm, action-free blanket cloth lined chore jackets. $2-3. [$5-15] *Fall/winter 1944-45*

Wat-a-tite poplin all-weather "Rainbreakers." Superb quality, highly mercerized. Durable finish that repels rain, snow, or sleet. Swagger fly front single breasted, or handsome officers' style in ivory tan. $14-19. [$5-15] *Fall/winter 1944-45*

Water repellent gabardine jacket, suede leather and wool loafer coat. $9-17. [$5-15] *Fall/winter 1944-45*

Handsome, well tailored topcoats of popular gabardine. Water repellent. Medium tan. $20-30. [$5-15] *Spring/summer 1945*

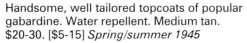

134

Cold weather caps in sport styles, made from warm, rugged materials. Available in Mackinaw red-and-black plaid or solid colors. $1-2. [$5-15] *Fall/winter 1945-46*

Two-piece Slicker Suit

Waterproof oiled slicker work clothes, in two-piece slicker suit. Triple-treated double thick black cotton slicker cloth, for absolute protection against water, oils, greases, and acids. Ideal for all working conditions. $4.50. [$5-15] *Fall/winter 1945-46*

A $1.88

B $1.88

C $3.88

Good quality hats. Wool felt with upper welt brim and slightly raised edge on top to help brim hold shape (medium gray, brown, dark gray, black), virgin wool felt with dressy bound edge, with split leather sweatband (medium gray, medium brown, medium blue), and genuine fur felt hat with plain edge, softer, richer, and longer wearing. Takes any shape you give it, crease it the way you like best (medium gray, medium brown, dark gray, black). $2-4. [$5-15] *Fall/winter 1945-46*

Shoes

Sears MILITARY STYLE Dress Shoes in 3 qualities

Western-type boots, preferred by Westerners. Double and triple soled styles, original "Chippewa" ranger shoes and boots. Available in black. $5-8. [$35-40] *Spring/summer 1944*

Sears military style dress shoes in three qualities. Finest Gold bonds with calfskin uppers are shiny and smooth. Gold bond quality with springy rubber heals and rugged leather soles. Sandy Nevin quality, already broken in. Smooth leather insoles, rubber heels, Goodyear welts. Regular military oxford style in brown and black, newest military oxford style in brown only. $4-7. [$20-30] *Fall/winter 1943-44*

Wear preflexed Sandy Nevins already broken in for old-shoe comfort from your first step. New wing tip, brown walled last, antiqued brown custom brogue, and double-duty work dress moccasin styles in brown leather available. $4-5. [$20-30] *Spring/summer 1944*

Johnson cushioned comfort shoes, four special styles that emphasize comfort... each with Johnson leather covered cushion. Strong steel shank supports your foot, rugged leather soles and rubber heels for long wear. $5. [$20-30] *Spring/summer 1944*

Dressy walled toe oxford, wing tip style, and double duty work or dress moccasins, all made of fine quality, rugged leather, and sporting long-wear rubber or tire-cord soles. Available in brown. Men's smart, cool ventilated dress oxfords. Step smartly in cool comfort in these smart Gold Bonds. Hundreds of perforations pump in the breezes with each step. Shape retaining, Gold Bond quality breathable leather. $5. [$20-30] *Spring/summer 1944*

Your best buy for farm and general outdoor wear. Double tanned leather work boots for the most service and wear. Goodyear welt, two soles, solid leather throughout. Made to resist barnyard soil and acids. $4-6. [$30-40] *Spring/summer 1944*

General utility boots with western features… lace-to-toe mill boots, oil tanned double soled, or oil tanned lace-to-toe 10-inch boot. Plump cowhide uppers treated to resist moisture. Specially designed for comfort in the workplace. $7-8. [$30-40]
Spring/summer 1944

Johnson Cushioned Comfort shoes and oxfords, just like walking on air. Styles for dress or work. Use your ration stamp. $7-8. [$30-40]
Fall/winter 1944-45

Men's low-cost-per-mile dress oxfords, sturdy and comfortable. Moc-style with rubber soles, or wing tip style, smooth leather uppers with husky rubber soles and smooth leather insoles for comfort. $2-3. [$20-30]
Spring/summer 1944

Sandy Nevin, Jrs., our finest boys shoes. Smart husky wing tip, saddle stitched moc style, brown military oxford styles. Brown and black. $3-4. [$15-25] *Fall/winter 1944-45*

Finest Gold Bonds, best leathers, lasts and workmanship. Choose them for a smoother fit, smarter style, and longer wear. Rationed. $6-8. [$20-30] *Fall/winter 1944-45*

Australian kangaroo leather for comfort and long wear. Dressy square toe oxford or wide toe blucher style. Goodyear welt leather soles, rubber heels. Black. $5-6. [$20-30] *Fall/winter 1944-45*

139

Thrifty Wearmasters give big value for the price. Strong double soles with tough "Compo" outsole and full Garrison backstay. Drill lined vamp and strong nailed construction. Available in black, use your ration stamp. $2-3. [$30-40] *Spring/summer 1945*

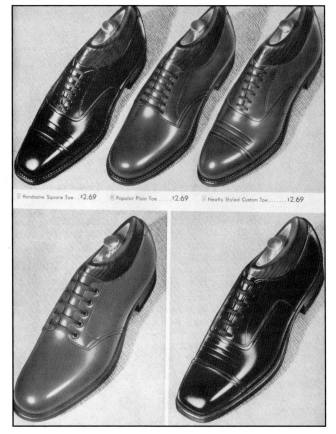

Handsome Square Toe....$2.69   Popular Plain Toe.....$2.69   Neatly Styled Custom Toe.......$2.69

Double-tanned Wearmasters, Goodyear welt construction. Choice of oil treated leather or tire-cord soles. Marine type shoes for extra service, "on the march" service and durability. $4-6. [$20-30] *Spring/summer 1945*

Briargate oxfords, with genuine Goodyear welt just like highest-priced shoes. Shoe flexes easily, holds shape longer, easier to resole. Handsome square toe, popular plain toe, neatly styled custom toe, brown or black military style and bright black square toe available. $2-4. [$20-30] *Spring/summer 1945*

Wearmasters safety steel toe shoes help prevent foot injury. $3-6. [$20-30] *Spring/summer 1945*

Cushioned-comfort Johnsons with five special foot relaxing features: heel-to-toe leather covered cushion absorbs jolts and jars, and helps lessen that tired, foot weary feeling after a day of active walking. Steel shank helps reinforce the shoe and holds up the arch of your foot. Extra flexible leather insole. Goodyear welt sewed leather soles, and cushiony rubber heels. $3-4. [$20-30] *Spring/summer 1945*

Sandy Nevins, built to take the wear of rough and tumble play. Extra husky moc style, no-mark rubber sole, popular moc style, black or brown dressier style moc. Designed for comfort and durability. Goodyear welt. $3. [$15-25] *Spring/summer 1945*

Teen Boys' Fashions

Dress Wear

Sears good looking, inexpensive suits for boys. Sturdy, long wearing wool mixed fabrics tailored in the latest styles. Navy blue cheviot, economy double breasted, sturdy hard finished worsted wool suits. Lined with rayon, smartly styled slacks and easy-fitting jackets. 3-piece single breasted, remarkably low priced. Fabric is smooth Cassimere with stylish wide herringbone weave. 2-piece suit trimly and attractively styled the way young men like them. Dressy, drape model slacks. Comes in medium blue and medium brown. $8-13. [$5-15] *Fall/winter 1943-44*

Fraternity Prep sports outfits… man–styled suits for older boys. All wool coats in plaids and solids. $12-15. [$5-15] *Spring/summer 1944*

All wool sports coats with calvary twill or smart gabardine slacks. Entire outfit: $12-15. [$5-15] *Fall/winter 1944-45*

Fraternity Prep expertly tailored, fine quality all wool spring suits. Smart patterns, youthful styles. Single or double breasted all wool herringbone, or virgin wool suiting. Sturdy for school, smart for "Sunday best." $12-16. [$5-15] *Spring/summer 1945*

Wool slacks in boys sizes. Herringbone tweed in medium brown or blue, patented Foreside pockets have a deep-down position for carrying valuables. All seams serged to prevent raveling. $5-6. [$5-15] *Fall/winter 1944-45*

Smart 2 piece suits and sport outfits... latest campus styles and fabrics for older boys. $11-14. [$5-15] *Spring/summer 1945*

Casual Clothing

Pilgrim NOBILITY Pullover Sweaters . . . All Wool

Our best quality . . . all heavyweight virgin yarns . . . either 100% zephyr wool (the softest kind of worsted) or zephyr wool mixed with lustrous mohair wool

Pilgrim Nobility pullover all wool sweaters. Made from zephyr wool and mohair, slightly napped for softness. Comes in solid patterns, ribbed style, and genuine Scotch Argyle. $4-6. [$10-20] *Fall/winter 1943-44*

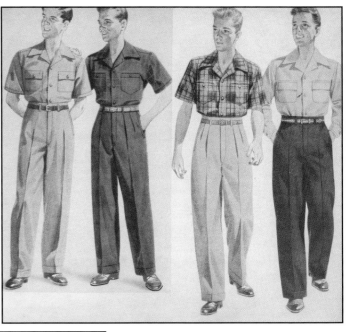

Boys' Fraternity Prep slack suits are cool and colorful, washable, and sanforized, too. Gabardine, cotton, and rayon fabric combinations, youthful tapering slacks have deep, full pleats, dropped belt loops, wide cuff bottoms. Shirts available in plaids or solids. $4-6. [$5-15] *Spring/summer 1944*

Pilgrim NOBILITY Coat Style Sweaters

Our finest quality because they're made 1. of softer yarns selected for their warmth, long wear, 2. with the greatest possible care in every detail, and 3. by a group of fine craftsmen, trained for years in tailoring the best grade of sweaters.

Pilgrim Nobility coat style wool sweaters. "Coat" front is all soft wool flannel, knit back and sleeves and napped. All zephyr wool worsted. English rib effect style available. Right rib stitches give easily. $5-8. [$30-40] *Fall/winter 1943-44*

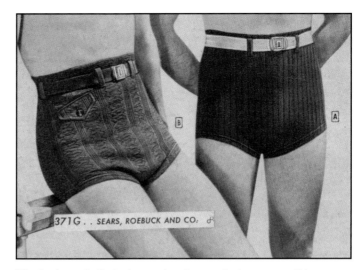

Pilgrim brand all virgin wool swim trunks in two qualities. Medium heavy worsted, knitted with the longest, strongest wool fibers. Stretchy and supportive. The heavy zephyr wool worsted trunks are as soft as can be. Navy blue, royal blue, and maroon. $2-3. [$25-35] *Spring/summer 1944*

Leisure coats styled for school or sports. Fraternity Prep tailored to give that casual, free-and-easy fit that "clicks" with style-minded Young America. Tweed-like all wool, rayon lined, and all wool two-tone styles in tannish brown and camel tan. $6-11. [$30-40] *Spring/summer 1944*

Here are the pullovers that are favorites with the young fellows and that will be seen in classrooms from coast to coast. They're knit of 100% wool yarns for warmth, carefully tailored. $3-5. [$5-15] *Fall/winter 1944-45*

Novelty check all wool or suede leather two-tone leisure coats. In brown or blue two-tone. Full lining of rich rayon, sateen lining in sleeves. $12-22. [$30-40] *Fall/winter 1944-45*

Sturdy Matched Outfits

Husky for work . . . neat enough for dress

Sturdy matched outfits, husky for work, neat enough for dress. $3-4. [$5-15] *Spring/summer 1945.*

Cool and colorful summer slack suits for boys. Custom tailored under Fraternity Prep label, made of cotton gabardine or crisp, cool poplin. Good looking and long wearing. $3-5. [$5-15] *Spring/summer 1945*

Good looking sweater coats. Smart checked front with zip closure, plain color sleeves, back and trim. Wool flannel front in plaid patterns, Nobility brand. Virgin wool worsted rib effect button front cardigan style. $4-8. [$30-40] *Spring/summer 1945.*

Outerwear

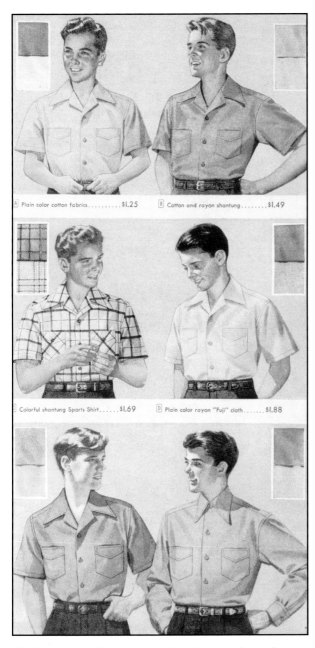

A) Plain color cotton fabrics..........$1.25   B) Cotton and rayon shantung........$1.49

C) Colorful shantung Sports Shirt......$1.69   D) Plain color rayon "Fuji" cloth.......$1.88

Our best gabardine sports shirts, long or short sleeve, in blue, tan, or sandune. $2-3. [$5-15] *Spring/summer 1945*

Sears all wool reversible and fraternity prep velofleece coats. Reverses to gabardine, or deeply quilted iridescent rayon lined. $8-14. [$5-15] *Fall/winter 1943-44*

Heavy all wool jackets. All wool with leather sleeves, smart panel front style, and low priced 33-ounce melton style. $7-15. [$30-40] Fall/winter 1943.

Fashion Tailored wool leisure coats, in handsome color combinations and high quality fabrics. Novelty checked sleeves. Styled in Hollywood for streamlined appearance, jaunty and modern, and designed for maximum comfort. Medium tan two-tone, medium brown two-tone, medium blue two-tone. $15-16. [$30-40] *Spring/summer 1944*

Style, protection, and warmth for active boys. Reversible Zelan-treated jackets to repel moisture. Made from army-type cotton poplin fabric. $2-6. [$10-20] *Spring/summer 1944*

148

Children's Fashions

Dresses and Suits

FLOCK DOT SHEER........$1.98   D JUMPER-EFFECT DRESS... $1.98   E TWO-TONED CHAMBRAY...$1.98

Smart KNICKER SUITS styled for growing boys

Roomy full cut sizes . . . rugged fabrics . . . strongly tailored throughout
All available on Sears Easy Terms, see inside back cover for details

Smart knicker suits styled for growing boys. Roomy full cut sizes… rugged fabrics. Boyville suits are exceptional values, and he'll be proud to wear it anywhere. Coat fully lined with lustrous rayon. Suits available in medium brown, medium gray, medium blue. $5-10. [$5-10] *Fall/winter 1943-44*

Washable cottons and luxable rayons for girls. Jumper-effect dress in sanforized percale and cotton sheen, dirndl skirt, two toner in woven chambray, gay striped yoke, ruffle, and full gathered skirt, two-piece suit in printed washable cotton, short cut-away jacket with bright embroidery, rayon peasant type jumper with dirndl skirt, pretty party dirndl in smooth spun rayon. $2 each. [$5-10] *Spring/summer 1944*

Low priced cottons for little girls, all washable. Dress up playsuit in checked cotton, thrift special of striped batiste, red, white 'n' blue dimity pinafore, sturdy chambray with striped trim, and sheer dimity with smocked bodice. $1. [$5-15] *Spring/summer 1944*

Boyville knee-length sock, genuine Jacquard cuff tops fit snugly over knicker cuffs. In brown or blue. 33¢ a pair, 3 for 97¢. [$2-5] *Fall/winter 1944-45*

Multi-color chambray, percale two-piecer, and flock dot sheer washable cotton dresses for girls. $2. [$5-10] *Spring/summer 1944*

Boyville Jr. loafer coats and slacks, in smart combinations just like dad's and big brother's. Dressy gabardine, sports style, or two-tone are sturdy and long wearing. $5-9. [$5-10] *Spring/summer 1945*

Knicker suits and raincoats by Boyville. Virgin wool tweed, all wool herringbone, wool and rayon blend. Full-cut knickers, fully lined coats. Tan tweed, medium blue, medium brown. $9-12. [$2-5] *Spring/summer 1945.*

Playwear

Corduroy for play or dress wear. Thickset, lined woven bib pants or longies. Jackets to match, in navy blue, green, maroon, or dark brown. $3-5. [$5-10] *Fall/winter 1943-44*

151

Fraternity Prep twin sweater sets, part wool, rayon, and cotton. Knit of all wool yarns in a wide panel rib. Ribbed bottoms give snug, neat fit. Wear together for real warmth, or wear only the sleeveless pullover alone or with a sportscoat for variety. Camel tan with luggage trim, or solid light blue and tan. $4-6. [$15-25] *Fall/winter 1943-44*

Super-quality deluxe Honeysuckles. Made of the finest fabrics, in the prettiest styles. $2. [$5-15] *Fall/winter 1943-44*

Wide selection of sturdy Playclothes

Available after August 1

Rollic all wool sweaters for little boys and girls. Cardigan knit styles with smart yokes and cute embroidery, in patriotic reds, whites, and blues. $2. [$2-10] *Fall/winter 1943-44*

Sturdy, inexpensive playclothes for active youngsters. Range king, Broncho girl, and Flying cadet, multiple piece outfits. Fun, bright colors and made to last for hours and hours of happy play. $2-3. [$25-50] *Fall/winter 1943-44*

152

Pinafores, blouses, and skirts. Washable cottons for teens, in striped percale, unbleached muslin with full gathered skirt, everglaze chintz, and checked cotton pinafore with embroidered pockets, red lacing trim, dirndl skirt. $1-2. [$2-5] *Spring/summer 1944*

Boys' rugged work or play suits. Lined bib suspenders, button front, made especially for hard wear, perfect for after school jobs or farm work. Army type fabric, tough army twill, sturdy work suits, husky cotton drill, in olive drab, tan, cadet blue, or suntan drill. $1-2. [$2-10] *Spring/summer 1944*

Sturdy playtogs for little ones. Washable cotton 2-piece slack suits, in cotton chambray, cotton crinkle crepe, and sturdy cotton twill. Button up overalls and sailor styles also available. $1-2. [$2-10] *Spring/summer 1944*

Boys, girls… wear the uniform of the service you like best! Army Officer's uniform, Jr. "WAC" outfit, Naval officer's uniform, Jr. "WAVE" outfit, or Sanforized Sailor suit, all in authentic greens, olives, blues, browns. $3. [$20-40] *Spring/summer 1944*

Flying officer's suit, officer's 2-tone, Naval officer's suit, button-on sailor suit, middy style sailor suit. $4-9. [$20-40] *Spring/summer 1944*

Smart and good-looking Military style uniforms for boys and girls. Sailor suits, chief petty officer, flying officer, whipcord breeches, 7-piece Range king, Jr. "WAC," and Army Officer's uniforms. $2-9. [$20-50] *Fall/winter 1944-45*

Wool, cotton and rayon satin twill swim trunks for boys. Adjustable drawstring waist. Maroon, royal blue, light blue, light tan, and maize. $1-2. [$2-5] *Spring/summer 1945*

Boyville knit polo shirts in colorful striped patterns. $1. [$5-10] *Spring/summer 1944*

Sweaters for big boys, checked front, pullover, all wool panel ribbed, and lightly brushed zephyr wool styles. Crew or V-neck. Camel tan, medium blue, maize, luggage brown. $3-4. [$5-15] *Spring/summer 1945*

Sweatshirts and pullovers, cotton and wool knit styles. Maize, blue, camel, luggage brown, maroon. $1-3. [$2-10] *Fall/winter 1944-45*

Sturdy, flat knit cotton sweatshirts, warm cotton fleecing inside. Double ribbed cuffs, neck, and bottom. $1. [$2-5] *Spring/summer 1945*

Boyville knit polo shirts for big and little boys. Bold, lively colors and patterns. $1-2. [$5-15] *Spring/summer 1945*

Girls love blouses spiced with new necklines, gay embroidery. $1-2. [$5-10] *Fall/winter 1945-46*

Shoes

Exceptional values in a variety of children's styles. Barefoot sandal, dress oxford, double tie, saddle oxford, original, or deluxe biltwel active shoe. $1-3. [$2-5] *Spring/summer 1944*

Little boys' school and play styles that take lots of wear. Soles of tough tire-cord, constructed of finest grade horsehide leather, or new non-marking brown rubber. $1-3. [$2-5] *Spring/summer 1945*

Outerwear

Warm heavy all wool Mackinaws. Plaid combinations, double breasted, fully lined with cotton flannel or Kasha. $4-6. [$5-10] *Fall/winter 1944-45*

Smart Boyville Jr. dress hats for little boys. Gabardine first kapper, 100% all wool flannel tam, all wool eton cap, or authentic gabardine Army officer cap with eagle emblem and metal stars and buttons. Each $1. [$2-10] *Spring/summer 1945*

Schoolgirls hats in varied styles at typical Sears low prices. $1-3. [$5-15] *Spring/summer 1945*

Spring coats in tailored classic styles, or all wool dress coats with soft lines and fine details, in light, bright springy colors. $4-9. [$2-10] *Spring/summer 1945*

Outdoor suits are treated to repel moisture. Extra warm because they have heavier, thicker linings. Gay all wool plaids with warm, fluffy lambskin lining. Army type zelan poplin coat, lamb-lined. $8-12. [$2-10] *Fall/winter 1945-46*

Suits and jackets in grade school sizes. Match them with all your clothes, and wear them everywhere! $6-12. [$5-10] *Fall/winter 1945-46*

Double-duty sets, smartly styled, well made coats to wear for school or dress-up, matching pants to slip on in colder weather. $13-16. [$2-10] *Fall/winter 1945-46*

Sleepwear and Underwear

Boyville cotton blanket robes. Beacon robe in gay, Indian blanket pattern, heavy-weight Whittenton softly napped cotton, or wrap around, double breasted style extra heavy Beacon robe. Blue, brown, maroon. $2-4. [$20-40] *Fall/winter 1943-44*

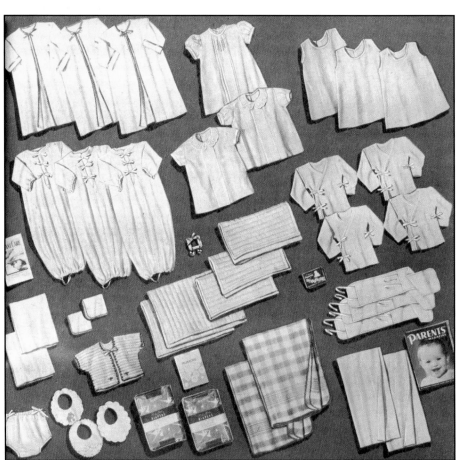

Sears deluxe complete 65 piece layette, including every piece every baby needs. Expertly detailed for longer better wear. Made from the softest fabrics and most comfortable, gentle styles. $18.75. [$30-50] *Spring/summer 1945*